MANIPULATED

ALEXANDER PAGANI

CHARISMA HOUSE

Manipulated by Alexander Pagani
Published by Charisma House, an imprint of Charisma Media
1150 Greenwood Blvd., Lake Mary, Florida 32746

Copyright © 2025 by Alexander Pagani. All rights reserved.

Unless otherwise noted, all Scripture quotations are taken from the *Holy Bible*, New Living Translation, copyright ©1996, 2004, 2015 by Tyndale House Foundation. Used by permission of Tyndale House Publishers, Carol Stream, Illinois 60188. All rights reserved.

Scripture quotations marked AMP are from the Amplified® Bible (AMP), Copyright © 2015 by The Lockman Foundation. Used by permission. www.Lockman.org

Scripture quotations marked ESV are from The ESV® Bible (The Holy Bible, English Standard Version®), copyright © 2001 by Crossway, a publishing ministry of Good News Publishers. Used by permission. All rights reserved.

Scripture quotations marked KJV are from the King James Version of the Bible.

Scripture quotations marked NIV are taken from the Holy Bible, New International Version®, NIV®. Copyright © 1973, 1978, 1984, 2011 by Biblica, Inc.® Used by permission of Zondervan. All rights reserved worldwide. www.zondervan.com. The "NIV" and "New International Version" are trademarks registered in the United States Patent and Trademark Office by Biblica, Inc.®

Scripture quotations marked NKJV are taken from the New King James Version®. Copyright © 1982 by Thomas Nelson. Used by permission. All rights reserved.

While the author has made every effort to provide accurate, up-to-date source information at the time of publication, statistics and other data are constantly updated. Neither the publisher nor the author assumes any responsibility for errors or for changes that occur after publication. Further, the publisher and author do not have any control over and do not assume any responsibility for third-party websites or their content.

For more resources like this, visit MyCharismaShop.com and the author's website at alexanderpagani.global.

Cataloging-in-Publication Data is on file with the Library of Congress.
International Standard Book Number: 978-1-63641-478-2
E-book ISBN: 978-1-63641-479-9

1 2025
Printed in the United States of America

Most Charisma Media products are available at special quantity discounts for bulk purchase for sales promotions, premiums, fundraising, and educational needs. For details, call us at (407) 333-0600 or visit our website at www.charismamedia.com.

CONTENTS

Introduction 1

Chapter 1   Rigid Rulemaking 7

Chapter 2   Judgmental Attitudes, Exclusivity, and Elitism 33

Chapter 3   Fear-Based Obedience 55

Chapter 4   Worshipping Tradition 71

Chapter 5   Misplaced Zeal and Rule-Free Righteousness 93

Chapter 6   Misuse of Authority 113

Chapter 7   Overemphasis on Appearance 129

Chapter 8   Resistance to Change 141

Chapter 9   Manipulating with Guilt and Shame 155

Chapter 10   Idolizing Old Testament Paradigms 173

Chapter 11   The Perfect Law of Liberty 191

Chapter 12   Say Goodbye to Bondage 207

A Personal Note from the Author 223

Notes 225

Special Thanks 229

About the Author 233

INTRODUCTION

I CLEARLY REMEMBER RUNNING down the street in 1998, frantically looking under every car for a gum wrapper I'd failed to throw in the public trash can. After more than fifteen minutes, I found it, and unspeakable joy (and relief) hit me. Why? Because I truly believed that if Christ returned before I properly disposed of that wrapper, I would not make it to heaven. My spiritual training said littering was not only lawbreaking; it was sin, and dying in my sin would have sent me to hell.

That might sound foolish to you, and you might be tempted to laugh at my line of thinking. But in my early walk with Christ (and for many years after that), thoughts like that plagued me—even through my nine-year prison term and long after my release. I had a condition I call OCRD, or obsessive-compulsive religious disorder. I was so afraid of not making the rapture that I kept apologizing and asking people I might have offended to forgive me. Gripped by the compulsion to walk in absolute holiness, I became miserable and mentally tormented, terrified to think the lake of fire would be my place of eternal unrest.

A system of belief controlled me—yes, *manipulated me.* Thank God for the freedom I found in Christ—but it took me ten or fifteen years to get there! Honestly, legalistic ideologies still trip me up at times. My wife, Ibelize, can detect my bouts with legalism, and she has helped me break out of them. So have the principles

I've outlined in this book. Applying them has moved me away from the toxicity of legalism and into the liberty with which Christ made me free.

Throughout these chapters, I will show you my real-life battle with legalism, and I will share the liberty I found. But first, let me explain legalism and its root.

What Is Legalism?

According to *Merriam-Webster*, *legalism* is a "strict, literal, or excessive conformity to the law or to a religious or moral code...a legal term or rule."[1] I can attest that in legalistic churches, the word *strict* is an understatement. I'm not saying these churches are without love; I'm saying their primary cultural expression is conformity to their religious code.

Legalism demands strict rules, prescribed ways of dealing with others, rigid bylaws, and more. In place of a Christianity built on vibrant relationship, there's a regimen of mechanical coercion. Instead of a proper exegesis of Scripture—noting the context, when the text was written, and to whom it was written—a blind literalism defines the reader's understanding and obedience. Believers in this setting are compelled to obey the text's literal form at all costs, often to the point of speaking, looking, and dressing like Old Testament figures.

The excessive conformity I just described controls a church's overall culture and silences the individual. Fierce conviction overshadows critical thinking, and no one dares challenge what the larger group has broadly accepted. This is called *groupthink*, "a pattern of thought characterized by self-deception, forced manufacture of consent, and conformity to group values and ethics."[2] In this type of corporate legalism, no one wants to be the oddball, so everyone goes with the herd. A powerful fear of rejection keeps legalism in place. It's the reason people stay in churches they know are toxic.

Does that mean holiness is wrong? No! Holiness couldn't possibly be wrong; our God is holy, we are called to be holy, and we are to worship the Lord in holiness. (See Leviticus 19:2; Deuteronomy 14:2; and Psalm 96:9.) But legalism is definitely wrong. So I am not equating holiness with legalism. Yet many believers trying to walk holy accept legalism as the standard. This misunderstanding can damage their faith, shipwreck their family and other relationships, and draw them away from the Lord and His church.

The apostle Paul dealt with legalism in the church at Collosae. People known as Judaizers followed Paul's apostolic missionary work and infiltrated the churches he founded, looking to force Gentile believers in Christ to accept the Jewish rite of circumcision. This ideology became a stronghold in the early church, and the Judaizers became known as "the circumcision."

In Acts 15 the church called a convocation to address this issue. At one point, the apostle Paul publicly refuted the hypocrisy of the apostle Peter, who had flip-flopped on this matter. (See Galatians 2:11–21.) In his letter to the church at Colossae, Paul explained the doctrinal and theological fallacies that drove the controversy:

> You have died with Christ, and he has set you free from the spiritual powers of this world. So why do you keep on following the rules of the world, such as, "Don't handle! Don't taste! Don't touch!"? Such rules are mere human teachings about things that deteriorate as we use them. These rules may seem wise because they require strong devotion, pious self-denial, and severe bodily discipline. But they provide no help in conquering a person's evil desires.
> —COLOSSIANS 2:20–23

Paul did not name holiness as a problem. He simply pointed out how rules and regulations were drawing the Colossians away from dependence on the person of Christ, His finished work on the cross, and the person of the Holy Spirit, while driving them toward human-based rules for Christian discipline. The church at

Collosae made the quality of their obedience the center point of their faith. This works-based gospel threatened to replace the faith-based gospel Paul (and of course Jesus) preached.

Without realizing it many believers who embrace a "holiness gospel" end up under the spell of a different spirit. As a result, they worship a different Jesus from the One they first followed. Anything that is not centered around the person of Jesus Christ or the efficacy of His work on the cross is legalism and not genuine biblical holiness. And anything that focuses more on what the believer does than on what Jesus has already done is not biblical Christianity; it is pietism!

Pietism is an "emphasis on devotional experience and practices; affectation of devotion."[3] If that doesn't describe hyperlegalism, I don't know what does! Among legalists there is a certain affection for the preaching of devotion instead of the preaching of Christ. I am not saying that legalists aren't preaching Christ at all, but they emphasize being *on fire* for Christ more than they stress *abiding in* Christ. Such preaching and teaching ultimately produce a toxic Christianity because legalism is inherently toxic. That is why Paul was so determined to address the matter in his epistles!

Many misunderstandings of Scripture can blind us, and legalism is one of them. The psalmist wrote, "Open my eyes to see the wonderful truths in your instructions" (Ps. 119:18). I urge you to pray this verse and humbly ask the Holy Spirit to give you the full understanding of all that you read in the coming chapters of this book. Then pray the prayer that follows this paragraph. Let the Holy Spirit give you mental clarity and convict you of any areas in which legalism has robbed the freedom Christ purchased for you. May the Spirit give you the strength to stand against legalism, even as you pray.

> *Lord Jesus, thank You for the cross and for purchasing my freedom from legalism. Thank You for sending the Comforter to help me walk in what You accomplished.*

Holy Spirit, as I read this book, I ask You to open my eyes to the dangers of legalism. Show me where it is affecting my life. Guide my steps as I totally depend on the Word as the source of truth. Show me the wonderful truths in Your instruction! Heavenly Father, give me strength to make whatever changes are necessary to stand fast in Christ, unentangled by yokes of bondage. I ask all this in Jesus' name. Amen.

Chapter 1

RIGID RULEMAKING

If I know that what I am doing is wrong, this shows that I agree that the law is good. So I am not the one doing wrong; it is sin living in me that does it.
—ROMANS 7:16–17

LEGALISM IS NOT the New Testament standard. But living for Jesus is not a rule-free joyride either. As Christians, we need to live by standards that distinguish us from the world. Rules and parameters keep society and the church from plunging into chaos. The Scriptures establish regulations that keep us from displeasing the Lord or opening the door to the demonic. This is why the New Testament says, "Come out from them and be separate, says the Lord. Touch no unclean thing, and I will receive you" (2 Cor. 6:17, NIV).

There are rules, and the Holy Spirit guides us. As we follow, God's rules lead us away from sin and help us not to stumble. But obeying rules is not the entirety of our Christian experience. We are called to activate our faith by walking in love. When we walk in love, we obey the rules, not mechanically but organically. As Paul wrote, "Love does no harm to a neighbor. Therefore, love is the fulfillment of the law" (Rom. 13:10, NIV).

Rules are meant to be protective rather than restrictive, especially until we are mature enough to live responsibly. If you still need a regular scolding to obey God's commands, you're not yet mature. As the apostle Paul explained, "The heir, as long as he is a child, differeth nothing from a servant, though he be lord of all; but is under tutors and governors until the time appointed of the father" (Gal. 4:1–2, KJV).

Rules are given not to manipulate believers but to help us grow in responsibility, stability, and accountability. They are not meant to incarcerate us but are designed to bring freedom. When natural parents see their children obeying the rules without needing to be reminded, the parents can lighten up on the supervision. They might even consider handing over the car keys and granting other privileges that require increased responsibility.

That is what God desires for the church. He is trying to take us to higher levels of kingdom responsibility. But when He finds us arguing and legalistically enforcing rules, our immaturity shows we're not ready. In fact, the legalism that's designed to restrict believers who aren't ready produces arrested development! In essence, the rules perpetuate our immaturity.

In one church or another, you've probably heard the recurring message that "something is coming" or (in the slightly less religious version) "something big is coming." The problem is that nothing ever comes. The church keeps chasing the carrot at the end of the stick, always striving but never obtaining. If we're totally honest, this pattern of endless delay is rampant in legalistic systems. Those who end up obtaining the promises are those who leave these environments and are often brutally criticized for doing so.

After I left my legalistic denomination, a certain pastor told me the same thing every time he saw me: "Pagani, you'll be back." It's been more than fifteen years since I left. I believe God told me to leave and never go back.

RULES FEED THE FLESH

Rules are meant not to destroy us but to mature us. The law was designed to show us our sin and sinful nature. That's it! Paul made clear in Galatians 3:21 that there is no conflict "between God's law and God's promises." He added this caution: "If the law could give us new life, we could be made right with God by obeying it" (Gal. 3:21). In other words, rules and regulations don't impart strength. They simply reveal our need for Jesus to save us and for the Holy Spirit to empower us to obey God.

If you dig a level deeper, you realize the law empowers sin. As bizarre as that statement seems, Paul unequivocally agreed and wrote this: "The law aroused these evil desires that produced a harvest of sinful deeds" (Rom. 7:5). The law strengthens the flesh! When someone tells you *not* to do something, the first thing you want is to do it! Why? Because no matter how much you discipline yourself, "the sinful nature is always hostile to God. It never did obey God's laws, and it never will" (Rom. 8:7).

Your carnal mind and sinful flesh will never fully submit to God. I wish I had learned this lesson thirty years ago, when I first got saved. Then, I might not have spent half of my Christian experience trying in all futility to submit my flesh to God's will. I did all that striving because week after week, I heard teachings about holiness and tried really hard to live holy. I even kept a calendar in the back of my Bible so I could mark off the days when I didn't lust in my mind. Once, I went thirty straight days without sinning in my mind. But on the thirty-first day, I messed up so bad that I condemned myself for a couple of weeks and brooded over how vile and unsaved I was. In retrospect the Holy Spirit may have been teaching me a lesson I had overlooked from 1 Corinthians 15. There Paul wrote, "The sting of death is sin; and the strength of sin is the law" (v. 56, KJV).

Paul understood this not only by revelation but by personal experience. He knew the law that condemned sin was the very thing that empowered sin. He wrote, "At one time I lived without understanding the law. But when I learned the command [or rule] not to covet, for instance, the power of sin came to life" (Rom. 7:9).

Here is what Paul was saying: As soon as the command came, the desire to disobey got stronger. This is the work of the flesh, and we will have flesh from now until Christ comes. Paul also wrote, "Sin used this command to arouse all kinds of covetous desires within me! *If there were no law, sin would not have that power*" (Rom. 7:8, emphasis added).

Did you see that? "Sin would not have that power"!

So many of us read these verses with blinders on our spiritual eyes. I sure did! When I used to read Romans 7:8, I totally missed it. Either I believed Paul's warning had no practical application in my life, or I explained it away by convincing myself Paul was entirely focused on the Law of Moses. But he was also addressing rules that churches or believers impose on themselves through legalism—which meant he was speaking to me.

Legalism Is Toxic; Grace Is a Gift

The reason I wrote this book is simple: Legalism is toxic. Therefore, I'm going to treat legalism like the nuclear radiation it is (metaphorically, of course). My message to the church is to run from legalism. Why? Because it contaminates the gospel of grace. So please forgive the bluntness of what I'm about to say: Some of the most miserable saints I know are trapped in legalism. That's not true in every case, but it's true way too often.

Let me ask you the question Paul asked: "Am I suggesting that the law of God is sinful?" (Rom. 7:7). Paul then answered his own question, saying, "Of course not! In fact, it was the law that showed me my sin. I would never have known that coveting is wrong if the law had not said, 'You must not covet'" (Rom. 7:7).

Hopefully, we have settled the idea that believers need standards. But sound standards and stifling legalism are two different things. Many believers are confusing them by not recognizing their respective sources. Godly standards come from the Spirit of Christ. Legalism comes from the traditions of men. Paul explained that the law, which is "holy and right and good," shows us "how terrible sin really is. It uses God's good commands for its own evil purposes" (Rom. 7:12–13). Legalism uses your good intentions and your desire to please God to strap you into an emotional roller coaster: You're happy when you obey the rules; you're miserable when you don't. Being spiritually bipolar is a real thing. I can say that because I was that. My family had to walk on eggshells in my presence. And I still find myself slipping back into minor legalism at times.

That's when I turn to Romans 7:14–23 and remind myself that the apostle Paul struggled, just as I do. In that amazing passage Paul said, "I am all too human, a slave to sin. I don't really understand myself, for I want to do what is right, but I don't do it. Instead, I do what I hate" (vv. 14–15). The Apostle to the Gentiles explained that he knew when he was doing wrong, and this proved his agreement that "the law is good" (v. 16). The conflict between his desire and his behavior made him realize he wasn't "the one doing wrong" because the culprit was "sin living in [him]" (v. 17).

Paul's struggle is our struggle. His words speak to our experience with both sin and the law. This statement from Paul captures the battle: "There is another power within me that is at war with my mind. This power makes me a slave to the sin that is still within me" (Rom. 7:23).

If you're in a fight with legalism, you are not alone. Your struggle is a human one, and Jesus is the answer. He can defeat legalism. Look at what Paul said!

> Oh, what a miserable person I am! Who will free me from this life that is dominated by sin and death? Thank God! The answer is in Jesus Christ our Lord. So, you see how it is: In my

> mind I really want to obey God's law, but because of my sinful nature I am a slave to sin.
> —Romans 7:24–25

Forgive yourself for being human, and thank God for Jesus! He is the source of your freedom. On the cross, He paid the price for your sins. He purchased your freedom, and He is your righteousness. Nothing you do or fail to do can earn you His favor or strip away His love. Everything that needed to be done about your sin was done by Jesus on Calvary.

To this day, Jesus offers a gospel of grace to those tired of trying to perform in order to please Him. Salvation comes by trusting in what He did, not what you do. Grace and His unmerited favor are gifts. In essence, God gives you what you don't deserve. This is what the apostle Paul preached to the Gentiles. He presented the gospel by means of grace, turning people to the Savior, Jesus Christ.

Doctrinal Idolatry

Legalism is stubborn. It causes many in the church to ignore everything I've just said (and even what Paul said) and remain trapped in doctrinal idolatry. Here's what I mean: A believer can cleave to a certain doctrine even when the Scriptures reveal it to be false. People enslaved to legalism remain faithful to questionable doctrines, no matter how many times God sends prophets, teachers, dreams, and visions warning them to flee legalism.

I recently heard an influential brother who leans toward Cessationism announce publicly that he is a "card-carrying Cessationist." I hope this gentleman has left himself open to having his view changed by God. Every one of us acts on what we believe to be true, but we're not infallible. As much as I love and preach deliverance, deliverance is not a hill I'm willing to die on. At the moment, I am fully persuaded that Christians can have demons if they open doors through willful sin or ignorant disobedience. But I leave room for God to change my mind. If He does, I won't idolize my doctrine; I will change my view to match what He reveals.

Doctrinal idolatry is a very real problem for Christians. I believe that many of the people in Jesus' day were stuck in it. Perhaps that is why He cried out, "Father, forgive them, for they don't know what they are doing" (Luke 23:34). Jesus knew what the people of Israel were steeped in, and He knew they couldn't see past it.

Jesus also knows what blinds us. So the Holy Spirit is asking right now, "Are you stuck in doctrinal idolatry?" Don't be too quick to say no. We have all identified ourselves in certain ways, saying things like, "I am Pentecostal from the top of my head to the soles of my feet," or, "I'm all about that holiness." It hurts to say this, but such statements usually come from people leaning toward idolizing the rules and regulations of their preferred denominations.

I confess! I was a die-hard Pentecostal, and I used to say such things. So here's my disclaimer: I am not saying that being a Cessationist or a Pentecostal is sinful. I respect my brethren who hold those views, and both camps are saved. I'm simply making a point: Unless we're willing to give God room to test or alter our preferences, we risk becoming doctrinal idolaters.

You Can't Make This Up

I never understood why believers remained in harsh, restrictive Christian environments. My wife, Ibelize, told me heartbreaking stories about growing up in church. Once, she was put on church discipline for three years because she trimmed her bangs. Three years of punishment sounds bizarre, but the rule she broke was based on the idea that a woman's long hair is her glory. (See 1 Corinthians 11:15.) Her church strongly believed that by trimming her hair, Ibelize was willfully cutting off her glory.

Because they were strictly devoted to their rules, the leaders of Ibelize's church did not think three years of discipline was extreme.

They simply required her to stop participating in various activities and functions for three years.

I remember asking Ibelize, "Didn't you think that was legalistic?"

She just nodded and said, "We had no idea what legalism was."

I asked her, "Why didn't you just leave that church?"

She answered, "Where was I going to go? It was a sin to leave your church."

Then I asked her, "What did you do for three years?"

"Nothing," she said. "I just attended church like normal and watched everyone else participate."

These are the kinds of rules that misrepresent God and cause believers to leave the church. It's no wonder that some turn away from the faith altogether and never return.

Don't Talk to Strangers

How does one get trapped in rules and regulations? The Bible says ensnarement begins with an idea. When we fail to submit our ideas and opinions to the rigorous filter of Scripture, we end up in strange realms that are "foreign," "unfamiliar," or "not known."[1]

The word *strange* can be applied to legalism, which is a doctrine foreign to the gospel of grace that Paul preached. The writer of the Book of Hebrews wrote about this and warned, "Do not be attracted by strange, new ideas. Your strength comes from God's grace, not from rules about food, which don't help those who follow them" (Heb. 13:9).

New ideas that don't line up with Scripture are strange, and we need to avoid them. We train our children to flee strangers who entice them. We say, "Don't talk to strangers! Just run!" That is exactly what the author of Hebrews told the Jewish believers to do: Run away from ideas that do not line up with Scripture.

Recently, I received an email from a family that was worried about their senior pastor possibly getting into an extreme version of legalism. He had started to teach that Christians should avoid the lust of the eyes by throwing away their TV sets. I told the people who contacted me to run from that church. I didn't play church politics by telling them to submit and pray for their pastor. No! I told them to take their family and leave. But I also told them to do it the right way: They needed to speak to the pastors and leadership and explain why they planned to find another church.

Legalism is a strange doctrine. It lures you into a strange car, kidnaps you from the gospel of Christ, and drives you to another gospel. Therefore, I won't mince my words: Legalism is a false gospel. No matter how much you dress it up as holiness, legalism is a strange idea, and it is incompatible with God's grace!

The strength to live holy doesn't come from the law. Remember what Hebrews 13:9 says: "Your strength comes from God's grace." You need to cut off legalism right from the beginning. If you don't, you will end up adding one law after another, and you'll become enslaved to a demonic spirit of religion. So pay attention: You're about to see that some rules and regulations are empowered by demons.

DOCTRINE OF DEMONS

Legalism overemphasizes rules and downplays obedience to the Holy Spirit's voice. It's an unholy fixation with the secondary rules we create to help us keep the primary rules God has established. But instead of helping us, these secondary rules keep us so focused on our pet regulations that we abandon God's commands.

Our secondary rules are birthed by ideas that aren't filtered through Scripture. They are man-made ideas that aren't inspired by the Spirit. The Holy Spirit has never inspired legalism. The Spirit has always been after one thing: the death of your flesh—not by regulation or behavior modification but by crucifixion.

> You have died with Christ, and he has set you free from the spiritual powers of this world. So why do you keep on following the rules of the world, such as, "Don't handle! Don't taste! Don't touch!"? Such rules are mere human teachings

about things that deteriorate as we use them. These rules may seem wise because they require strong devotion, pious self-denial, and severe bodily discipline. But they provide no help in conquering a person's evil desires.

—Colossians 2:20–23

Paul is unambiguous about rules such as *don't touch* and *don't taste*. They give the appearance of godly wisdom but do nothing to kill ungodly desires. Paul is not telling us to abandon all rules. He's not saying we should handle everything because we are under grace. No. He is saying that our rules can become ridiculous and extreme, like the pastor who told believers to throw out their television sets. He added his ideas to what God said, and he became like Eve, who told the serpent in the garden that God said not to touch the tree of the knowledge of good and evil, when God simply said not to eat from that tree. (See Genesis 2:16–17; 3:3.)

I'm guessing Adam and Eve added the *don't touch* rule to keep themselves from eating the forbidden fruit. But Paul was right—such rules "provide no help in conquering a person's evil desires" (Col. 2:23). In the end Eve ate the fruit, and so did Adam!

Our rules don't kill ungodly desire, because they aren't inspired by God! When God's Word tells us to avoid something, the Holy Spirit empowers us to obey. The Holy Spirit is not obligated to empower our ideas. That's why no matter how many rules legalistic denominations put in place, their faithful followers break them.

We need to focus on Christ alone. He is our sufficiency. Paul said it this way: "So you also are complete through your union with Christ, who is the head over every ruler and authority" (Col. 2:10). We are complete in Christ. All we need is to believe that Christ, the living Word, is our sufficiency. Therefore, what is written is enough. If we forget that and cleave to rules and regulations that are self-imposed or denominational, we will run into issues and create another problem by sidestepping.

SIDESTEPPING

Yes, there is a sin against God's Word, and Jesus used the word *sidestep* to describe it. Carefully read the following passage from Mark's Gospel, and allow it to permeate your theological worldview.

> The Pharisees and teachers of religious law asked him, "Why don't your disciples follow our age-old tradition? They eat without first performing the hand-washing ceremony." Jesus replied, "You hypocrites! Isaiah was right when he prophesied about you, for he wrote, 'These people honor me with their lips, but their hearts are far from me. Their worship is a farce, for they teach man-made ideas as commands from God.' For you ignore God's law and substitute your own tradition." Then he said, "You skillfully *sidestep* God's law in order to hold on to your own tradition."
>
> —MARK 7:5–9, EMPHASIS ADDED

Jesus spoke powerfully, showing us how our views can trick us into sidestepping the Scriptures. It's a way of moving forward while ignoring something along the path. Just writing about this makes me tremble because I remember sidestepping many times when the Holy Spirit challenged me to break the rules and help somebody. But I ignored His voice and continued following my rules.

The parable of the good Samaritan is a great example of sidestepping. (See Luke 10:30–37.) A Jewish man had been attacked by bandits and left for dead on the road to Jericho.

> By chance a [Temple] priest came along. But when he saw the man lying there, he crossed to the other side of the road and passed him by. A [Levite] Temple assistant walked over and looked at him lying there, but he also passed by on the other side. Then a despised Samaritan came along, and when he saw the man, he felt compassion for him.
>
> —LUKE 10:31–33

Two other Jews who supposedly knew God's Word saw the man but did not help him. One was a priest who crossed the street in order to avoid him. Another was a priest's assistant (a temple Levite) who at least looked at the man but did nothing. Both men ultimately sidestepped compassion and went on their way.

In Mark 7 Jesus confronted the Pharisees for sidestepping God's commandments, which is exactly what the two men did in leaving a wounded man to die. In my opinion these men perfectly depict the legalistic church. They were concerned about following the rules to keep themselves pure so they could administer their duties in the temple. Legally, they were right about what helping the man would cost them. But morally they were dead wrong because they failed to love their neighbor.

This kind of error is so common in legalistic churches. Legalism keeps our eyes on the rules but blinds us to souls in need. It sacrifices the heartbeat of God's love for the sake of coldhearted rule enforcement!

In my early days of pastoring, I was young and naive. My children were very young, and Ibelize stayed home with them while I led our midweek Bible study. When service ended late that night, I was left alone with a pregnant church member. She obviously needed a ride home, but instead of allowing love to dominate me, I allowed a rule to bind me. It's a good rule about pastors never being alone with someone of the opposite sex. But my devotion to the rule and to appearances kept me focused on having a clear conscience and making sure I wasn't alone with a female.

So instead of offering to drive the pregnant woman home, I called a taxi, which was fine. But I didn't even have the courtesy to pay the fare. Completely entangled in avoiding any sense of impropriety, I simply waited for the taxi to arrive, made sure she got safely into the cab, and went home.

In other words, I sidestepped, just as the temple Levite did in Luke chapter 10. I could have easily called my wife to tell her I was giving the woman a lift home. Then my wife would have asked me to put her on the car's speaker, and she would have talked to the young lady while I drove. There would have been integrity, but without all the maneuvering.

I Hate You, but I Love You

Many people trapped in legalism have a love-hate relationship with the dogma they observe. They are grateful to their churches and thankful that someone led them to Christ. They appreciate learning the disciplines of Bible reading, prayer, fasting, and passionately seeking God. And they have been blessed to learn the principles of serving. Yet many of these grateful people also feel frustrated and trapped by rigorous routines—in some cases for decades. Some have not grown very much in the knowledge of Christ and the deeper things of the Word. Internally, they harbor resentment for the system that has held them, especially when they visit other congregations that are thriving in the things of God.

I remember being in a denominational church and doing street evangelism with other church members. When souls were won to Christ, we sent them to other churches because we knew they wouldn't grow in our church and would potentially backslide. I stayed in that denomination because I genuinely loved my pastor, and I knew he needed my help. I didn't want to abandon him, but I would go home to my wife feeling angry and resentful. There were seasons when I would cry and cry and cry because I felt trapped and didn't want to commit the dreaded sin of church hopping.

Does this scenario sound familiar? Do you hate the legalism of your church but love your pastors? It reminds me of the opposing feelings God had for brothers Esau and Jacob. "As it is written, Jacob have I loved, but Esau have I hated" (Rom. 9:13, KJV). I believe what God hated was not Esau but Esau's lack of concern for spiritual matters—much the way we can love the brethren who helped us get saved but hate the system that governs them.

It took me many years to let go and forgive my denomination.

But just as Jesus forgave those who had no clue what they were doing, I came to realize that the leaders I resented acted not out of malice but out of ignorance.

As you read this, allow the Holy Spirit to bring to your remembrance all the pain, resentment, and even offense that you suffered in a legalistic system. Ask the Holy Spirit to help you forgive—and do it now! I know they did you wrong and overlooked your investment in the church's vision. I understand how they abandoned and even erased you when you voiced minor disagreements. I've been there.

Maybe you were hurt in a different way. Maybe you were unchurched and showed some interest in the things of God but felt judged by a legalistic church or believer. As a result, you chose never to seek God or attend a church again.

Whatever hurtful, legalistic situation you faced, you're probably weeping as you read this page. Yet you must forgive and refuse to use the hurt you suffered at church as an excuse for not giving your life to Christ. Forgiveness is a choice, not a feeling. The feelings come only after you choose to forgive. Ephesians 4:32 tells us, "Be kind to each other, tenderhearted, forgiving one another, just as God through Christ has forgiven you." That is how healing comes.

Now pray this prayer aloud:

> *Heavenly Father, You know I am hurting because of what happened with* [name the people or church]. *I didn't deserve to be treated that way, and I've been offended ever since. But today I ask You to help me forgive them because You forgave me of many sins. I choose to release all offense because Jesus took my pain and hurts on the cross when He died for me.* [Now pray in your own words, as the Holy Spirit directs.] *I ask You all these things in Jesus' name! Amen.*

CONCESSIONS AREN'T DOCTRINES

The idea of concessions might be new to you. It took me a long time to understand it, but when I did, it changed my view about certain taboo subjects raised not only in religious churches but in the faith overall. *Concession* is "the act of conceding or yielding" a right, privilege, or point in an argument in order to make a situation less difficult.[2]

A concession can be a rule that is temporarily allowed under special circumstances. Remember that certain rules and restrictions in Scripture were not direct commands from the Lord. Some rules were established due to localized patterns of error that threatened to permeate the larger church. So a rule was used to stop the spread until more clarity could be given.

The same thing happens in modern times. I believe some of the legalism common in the United States resulted from the "free sex" and "hippie" movements of the 1960s. Pastors tried to help their members break free from these sins and made concessions in regard to external holiness. And guess what? It worked! We found that many who came out of those movements began to reflect Christlike modesty.

Yet something happened after that. Once the issue had been addressed, the concession was meant to be lifted. Out of fear, however, many pastors and leaders made the concession into dogma. The result was the legalism we see today.

Jesus acknowledged a concession in Matthew 19:8, when He said, "Moses permitted divorce only as a concession to your hard hearts, but it was not what God had originally intended." Notice permitting divorce was not God's original intent. The concession was a kind of temporary adjustment made because the people's hearts were hard (and would presumably soften in time).

Here's a contemporary example: I believe that God gives us dating opportunities so we can find someone suitable to marry. For safety's sake couples might ask to be chaperoned, or they might arrange for double dates to ensure they don't fall into sinful behavior. Are these restrictions scripturally mandated? No, but they can be wise concessions. For millennia, the devil has tempted unmarried couples to fornicate, resulting in countless unplanned pregnancies, forced or loveless marriages, and other miseries.

Before I married, I was sometimes alone late at night with a member of the opposite sex. I can say with a clear conscience that I never sinned in such situations. However, I don't recommend following my example. God intends for single people to get to know each other and see whether He wants them to pursue a serious relationship together. He allows dating concessions because of the hardness of our hearts.

When the COVID-19 pandemic hit New York City in 2020, everything changed for the church. It was also an election year and a season of civil unrest over the police brutality that killed George Floyd. I remember how intense things were within our multicultural community. To maintain the church's integrity, I had to make some concessions. One was to require everyone to respect everyone else's political affiliations. Church leaders were not permitted to discuss politics and would be stripped of their positions if they did. Political shaming was off-limits, and members were not to criticize one another for wearing or not wearing face masks.

The concession worked. For three years we had no problems among members, except for two people who left. New Yorkers are bold and brash when expressing themselves, and the concessions helped establish boundaries. When the pandemic ended, I dissolved the concessions, and we returned to pre-COVID normalcy.

Concessions Aren't Commands

Concessions are not commands. Addressing sexual and marital issues, Paul counseled husbands and wives in some detail. Notice, however, what he added: "I say this as a concession, not as a command. But I wish everyone were single, just as I am. Yet each person has a special gift from God, of one kind or another" (1 Cor. 7:6–7). Paul desired everyone to be single like him so they could dedicate themselves completely to the Lord. But this was a personal suggestion, and obeying it was optional.

Obeying commands is not discretionary. The question is, How many rules (concessions) are being enforced in churches as though they were commands? Concessions need to be reevaluated and possibly expunged. For example, my personal conviction is that we need to stop seating men on one side of the church and women on the other. Separating men and women was a concession established in a certain culture at a particular time. But we are in a different culture and time. This practice keeps husbands, wives, and children from worshipping together. A man's family needs to see him honoring God in worship and service in the kingdom. Let's prayerfully reconsider!

Our Brothers' Keepers, Not Policemen

In Genesis 4:9, when God asked Cain where his brother, Abel, was, Cain answered, "Am I my brother's keeper?" (KJV). God did address Cain's question, but scriptures such as Matthew 25:35–36 urge us to care for one another. The apostle Paul wrote, "Don't look out only for your own interests, but take an interest in others, too" (Phil. 2:4). And the following passage from Acts shows how the early church lived:

> They worshiped together at the Temple each day, met in homes for the Lord's Supper, and shared their meals with great joy and generosity—all the while praising God and enjoying the goodwill of all the people. And each day the Lord added to their fellowship those who were being saved.
>
> —Acts 2:46–47

The church wasn't socialistic but caring, and I believe this helped the church grow exponentially. Many churches model this kind of caring today. However, some churches develop a policing culture in which the brethren are busy looking for those violating the rules.

My mother-in-law experienced a policing church when she converted to Christ and joined the congregation in which my wife grew up. A woman in leadership actually assigned my mother-in-law to spy on the women of the church and report any violations so the women could be corrected. As disturbing as it was to me, I realized this very thing happened in the first-century church, as Paul explained:

> Even that question came up only because of some so-called believers there—false ones, really—who were secretly brought in. They sneaked in to spy on us and take away the freedom we have in Christ Jesus. They wanted to enslave us and force us to follow their Jewish regulations.
>
> —GALATIANS 2:4

Rule-based approaches overtake people who then justify malicious acts that were supposedly for the greater good. But that is nothing more than toxic, sneaky, and deceptive legalism. If any Christian movement or person asks you to police God's people, you need to flee. The apostle Peter said, "Don't lord it over the people assigned to your care but lead them by your own good example" (1 Pet. 5:3).

Being your brothers' keeper does not mean policing them. Policing makes you a faultfinder and critic who sees only the flaws in others. Jesus had strong words to say about that!

> How can you think of saying to your friend, "Let me help you get rid of that speck in your eye," when you can't see past the log in your own eye? Hypocrite! First get rid of the log in your own eye; then you will see well enough to deal with the speck in your friend's eye.
>
> —MATTHEW 7:4–5

Believers spying on other believers (including through social media platforms) happens when grace and law are mixed together in the church. This creates a new species of Christianity that God never intended. This mixture is unclean and unfit for the Master's service.

MIXED COVENANTS

How does mixture creep into the church? I believe it's a matter of failing to upgrade the old while stepping into the new. Please notice that I didn't say to abandon what is old. We don't abandon the Old Testament laws; but Jesus came to upgrade them. Holiness is still right, but the grace of God now teaches us to abstain from worldly lusts. (See Titus 3:3–7.) If we ignore the upgrades, we end up with mixture, which can go very wrong. Look at what Paul said about starting with grace but trying to mix in the law:

> Oh, foolish Galatians! Who has cast an evil spell on you? For the meaning of Jesus Christ's death was made as clear to you as if you had seen a picture of his death on the cross. Let me ask you this one question: Did you receive the Holy Spirit by obeying the law of Moses? Of course not! You received the Spirit because you believed the message you heard about Christ. How foolish can you be? After starting your new lives in the Spirit, why are you now trying to become perfect by your own human effort?
>
> —GALATIANS 3:1–3

Paul condemned this type of Christianity, so why are many believers still embracing it? Paul worked to realign the circumcision—the Jewish believers in Messiah who compelled Gentile believers to be circumcised. This was a mixture of the Old and New Testaments. But neither the gospel of Christ nor the Old Testament system tolerated mixture. Leviticus 19:19 states, "You must obey all my decrees. Do not mate two different kinds of animals. Do not plant your field with two different kinds of seed. Do not wear clothing woven from two different kinds of thread."

Have you ever wondered why mixing fabrics was an issue? Well, now you know: It was, at least in part, a warning in type and shadow about the mixture that would contaminate the future church. The gospel must remain in its purest form. Adding to it produces a different "gospel" with a different "Jesus." (See Galatians 1.) The early church condemned mixture in a variety of ways. Adding anything to the gospel makes it not the gospel of Christ but the gospel according to whatever person made the rules.

Paul's take was simple: If you're going to mix covenants, you might as well keep the whole law. He bluntly said,

> If you are trying to find favor with God by being circumcised, you must obey every regulation in the whole law of Moses. For if you are trying to make yourselves right with God by keeping the law, you have been cut off from Christ! You have fallen away from God's grace.
> —GALATIANS 5:3–4

In other words, steer clear of mixture!

Religious PTSD: Pressure to Submit Disorder

A mixed gospel can only lead to what I call religious PTSD: the "pressure to submit disorder" that is caused by legalism. My wife devised this concept to explain how she and her friends left their church with religious PTSD. The pressure to submit to the rules can be traumatizing, especially when no sin is involved, and the rule lacks God's heart.

Anyone can feel pressured to conform; even the apostle Paul briefly succumbed for the sake of peace. It happened when Paul wanted Timothy to join him on his second missionary journey. "In deference to the Jews of the area, he arranged for Timothy to be circumcised before they left, for everyone knew that his [Timothy's] father was a Greek" (Acts 16:3).

Imagine forcing a grown man to be circumcised just to please religious folks! The physical procedure must have been traumatic for Timothy; but even more traumatizing is the idea of being forced to submit. This was pure legalism. At one point, the church in Jerusalem told Paul, "The Jewish believers here in Jerusalem have been told that you are teaching all the Jews who live among the Gentiles to turn their backs on the laws of Moses" (Acts 21:21). They wanted Paul to shave his head in a purification ceremony to disprove this allegation, and Paul complied (I would speculate that Paul dealt with some religious PTSD himself). But I suspect the epistles he later wrote show how fed up he was with pressure from religious Jews.

Paul must have been a very patient man to conform to rigorous rules for the sake of the gospel. But conformity can also be driven by fear and the desire for acceptance. Experts say that "conformity is a type of social influence involving a change in belief or behavior in order to fit in with a group."[3] This is a powerful motive. You might not believe some of the dogma and bylaws of your church, but because you love the church and want to fit in, you conform.

That is exactly what I did for many years. In order to pass my classes in my denomination's Bible school, I had to agree with the school's established teaching. I didn't believe half of their extreme dogma, but I desperately wanted my ministerial credentials. After complying for many years, I became exhausted and expressed my displeasure with the denomination's works-based theology. That's when I was labeled a troublemaker (a story for another time).

The pressure to submit to the rules can cause some believers significant mental distress and fears about going to hell or being judged by the church or another believer. Countless believers who come out of legalism have the symptoms of religious PTSD. The pressure to conform can make the most upright people bend a knee.

Religious PTSD can also have the opposite effect, causing some people to rebel against the church. Many plunge deep into sin, as though they had never been raised in church. Some very hardened sinners have lost their way because of religious PTSD, and many end up lost in hell. This includes gifted musicians whose talent was discovered as they worshipped Jesus in the church. Yet now they are singing for Lucifer!

If you used to be a Christan and can identify with the realities of religious PTSD, I want to tell you something: Not all believers are willing to force rules and regulations down your throat. Extreme legalists don't represent the majority of believers in Christ. So please come back home; come back to Jesus. The Lord is waiting for you, and it's never too late to embrace the cross again.

I have a great burden for people dealing with religious PTSD. If that names you, the Holy Spirit can heal you. I would love to hear your story and possibly pray with you via email at info@alexander-pagani.global. Or you can learn to break free from religious PTSD by looking us up on social media or visiting our YouTube channel at Alexander Pagani LIVE (@alexanderpaganilive).

Citizens Who Mingle and Enjoy Life

It is curious to me that a hermit is someone who "retires from society and lives in solitude especially for religious reasons."[4] God did not call believers to be separated from the world and bound by man-made rules. Jesus wants us to go into the world and preach the gospel. Hermits don't evangelize in person; they become isolated and don't mingle with those who need Jesus. They might evangelize through social media, but that's mostly like preaching in an echo chamber.

Instead of being a light in the darkness, hermits hide out in the world. Jesus, the apostle Paul, and the early church commanded us to preach the gospel to every creature and take the gospel to the far corners of the earth. We can do that without fear of being contaminated by the world system. We are in this world, but we are not of this world. (See John 17:14–18.) We are to be "like a city on a hilltop that cannot be hidden" (Matt. 5:14), a light shining in a dark world. God wants the lost to notice us and hear us preach the gospel of Jesus Christ to them. We can do this and remain citizens of the kingdom, "along with all of God's holy people....members of God's family" (Eph. 2:19).

Jesus made us kingdom citizens, with kingdom rights. We go out to the world knowing we are not from around here, but our citizenship is from the heavenly Jerusalem. Therefore, we walk in the power of the Holy Spirit and have no reason to hide. This is why I disagree with the Amish movement, for example; I don't see isolation theology and separation culture as scriptural options.

Jesus has called us to walk in liberty and serve God without fear. I truly believe that God wants His people to enjoy life, sports, clean comedy, walks in the park, and family fun. Solomon concluded that "there is nothing better than to be happy and enjoy ourselves as long as we can. And people should eat and drink and enjoy the fruits of their labor, for these are gifts from God" (Eccles. 3:12–13).

Good, clean fun is allowed to us. So why did my wife's church teach her that riding a bike is a sin? Why was she prohibited from swimming in a public pool? I know the New Testament shows Jesus' twelve disciples only doing ministry. But I cannot imagine Jesus never having fun with them on a day off from ministry. Enjoying the life God gives us is good and godly.

Not Condemnation but Reconciliation

Let's not join the condemnation camp in these last days. Many zealous younger believers are using their online platforms to condemn people whose perspectives differ from theirs. This is not pleasing to Christ or inspired by the Spirit of God. "God has given us [the] task of reconciling people to him" (2 Cor. 5:18). And "if there was glory in the ministry of condemnation, the ministry of righteousness must far exceed it in glory" (2 Cor. 3:9, ESV).

The ministry of condemnation is alive and well, millennia after Moses received the Ten Commandments. But we are not called to condemn or exonerate anyone. Our job is to bring people back to God by preaching the death, burial, and resurrection of Jesus Christ. (See 1 Corinthians 15:1–4.) He paid the price and freed us from the cloud of condemnation. Paul made this point so clearly in Romans 8:1, saying, "So now there is no condemnation for those who belong to Christ Jesus."

Because of what Christ did, what truly matters is the new creation. When you have a revelation that you (and others) are a new creation in Christ, you know that your actions or failure to act can't change that. This truth revolutionizes how you see yourself and others, and it makes condemnation obsolete. Whether you are circumcised or not, submitted to bylaws or not, conversion means the Holy Spirit transformed you. Neither you nor anyone else gets to judge you or revoke what the Holy Spirit has done. Paul wrote, "It doesn't matter whether we have been circumcised or not. What counts is whether we have been transformed into a new creation" (Gal. 6:15).

Once I saw myself as a new creation, I could see others the same way, and my interaction with them was filled with respect and appreciation rather than criticism. Instead of being concerned about whether they were obeying a list of rules, I was moved by the revelation of the new creation. Rather than looking for external cues, I saw myself and others as God sees us—justified through Christ. Salvation is that good—and it is more than enough.

The New Creation, Abiding in Christ

The apostle Paul described the new creation in simple but powerful words:

> If any man be in Christ, he is a new creature: old things are passed away; behold, all things are become new. And all

> things are of God, who hath reconciled us to himself by Jesus Christ, and hath given to us the ministry of reconciliation.
> —2 Corinthians 5:17–18, kjv

When your worldview includes the new creation, you become free to colabor with Christ, moving toward a ministry of reconciliation and away from condemnation. This affects your speech and even your tone, which can bring people in and not repel them. So many believers overlook the second half of 2 Corinthians 5:18. (I know I did—for years.) It's as though the verse is hidden from view. Yet it's vital: God gave us the ministry of reconciliation. We have all been commissioned to bring people back to Christ; provide solutions-based, scriptural messages; and not con people when they don't measure up.

You become who or what you dwell on. If you dwell on Old Testament biblical personalities more than on Jesus, your life will be patterned accordingly. But if you make it your business to abide in Jesus, your theology will become less legalistic. In John 15:4 Jesus promised to abide in you when you abide in Him. This abiding makes you become more like Him. Why abide in another biblical personality when He is the One who God sent to us? He is the One the world awaited!

Abiding in Christ is essential. Meditating on the passage below will cause you to internalize the verses, and they will produce change in you.

> Yes, I am the vine; you are the branches. Those who remain in me, and I in them, will produce much fruit. For apart from me you can do nothing. Anyone who does not remain in me is thrown away like a useless branch and withers. Such branches are gathered into a pile to be burned. But if you remain in me and my words remain in you, you may ask for anything you want, and it will be granted! When you produce much fruit, you are my true disciples. This brings great glory to my father.
> —John 15:5–8

You may have read this passage thousands of times and heard countless sermons preached from it. But please read it again, with an eye to getting free from legalism. Many believers abide in Christ through salvation but don't really allow Him to abide in them through sanctification. If that is you, just allow Christ to abide in you. Then His Word will be strong in you, you will see prayers being answered, and you will produce fruit that remains.

Following a list of dos and don'ts cannot do these things for you. Rules are not inherently bad. But when they become the main thing, you need to detox and cleave to Christ. Let the Holy Spirit show you the rules and regulations that don't please Him. Reformers such as Martin Luther and John Calvin went through this process. You too can ask the Holy Spirit tough questions about why certain rules were initiated, and He will reveal any that are hindering God's work in your life. Have no fear; the Holy Spirit is guiding you!

Breaking Free and Moving Forward

Breaking free from a rule-based theology takes time, but it's worth it. Think of it as a sort of reprogramming in a more scripturally accurate way. The process advances not through quick solutions that serve as Band-Aids but through understanding and a revelation from God of the new creation. When you understand that people are truly born again and regenerated through the Holy Spirit, you realize what truly matters, and your life begins moving toward what God intended and what you have yet to see.

Chapter 2

JUDGMENTAL ATTITUDES, EXCLUSIVITY, AND ELITISM

Then they cursed him and said, "You are his disciple, but we are disciples of Moses! We know God spoke to Moses, but we don't even know where this man comes from."
—John 9:28–29

It is virtually guaranteed: You are who you sit under. You are who you continuously talk or preach about. You are the person around whom you pattern your life. Unless something changes, that person is the center of your focus, and you are that person's disciple.

Knowing that our focus in the Christian church is Christ, it might seem hard to believe that any other person could usurp His place. Yet it happens in some hyper-Pentecostal, Charismatic, and other churches where people led to faith in Christ are quickly directed toward a Moses-oriented discipleship. Instead of hearing about denying themselves and carrying their crosses daily, they're told to pursue the fire of God or the *shekinah*, as Moses did. Many church buildings even copy the appearance of the wilderness tabernacle, with the ark of the covenant behind the pulpit, shofar and oil in the pulpit, and curtains on the back wall of the platform.

And don't forget the large letters on the pulpit wall that declare, "Holiness unto the Lord."

Sunday after Sunday, certain churches emphasize the idea of being found faithful like Moses. Meanwhile, they preach the cross as an addendum rather than the main message. I was guilty of this in the early days of my pastorate. Whenever someone challenged my legalism, I offered the standard reply of every legalistic person: "I am not religious!"

Most Christians make this declaration at times, but those who pride themselves in being Spirit-filled or Charismatic say it the most. As denials go, this one is often far from true. Some of the most intolerant, legalistic believers claim not to be religious. You could say they are legalistic about *not* being legalistic. The reason is simple: Most churches given to legalism don't even know it. Yet their church cultures are based on unbearable systems of rules and regulations that are touted as discipleship but more closely resemble the burdensome Law of Moses.

Many of today's Christian influencers come from a pedigree of solid churches and ministers. That is not my story, however. My wife and I come from some of the harshest and most abusive spiritual environments you can imagine. In all honesty, they were cultish.

That is exactly why I wrote this book: to expose the dangers of real Christians becoming disciples of Moses. This issue surfaced during Jesus' earthly ministry. When Jewish leaders questioned a man Jesus healed from blindness, the man's answers about the miracle riled them. "Then they cursed him and said, 'You are his disciple, but we are disciples of Moses! We know God spoke to Moses, but we don't even know where this man comes from'" (John 9:28–29).

Of course they were disciples of Moses at that time, but their allegiance to Moses was so rigid they rejected the Messiah that Moses prophesied in Deuteronomy 18:15. The Jewish leaders cursed what seemed different from Moses's version of serving God. Moses's version was not bad or wrong, but its time was passing, and it paled in comparison to Jesus' ministry. Yet Jewish leaders were unwilling to hear Jesus.

The behavior of the Jewish leaders is common in modern legalistic settings where the leaven of Moses—a combination of judgmentalism, exclusivity, and elitism—is prevalent. This type of legalism's core is veneration. The leaders who found the blind man's healing disturbing venerated Moses almost to the point of deifying him. Their focus on Moses blinded them to the divine presence in their midst.

We naturally tend to venerate those who help shape our lives. But like the children of Israel who resisted Jesus, we can end up cursing what is good and holy. That is what veneration often does. It opposes anyone who is different from the one we're venerating. It borders on human idolatry.

VENERATION VERSUS IDOLATRY

There is a difference between veneration and idolatry. No one in their right mind would embrace human idolatry knowing the judgment it brings. But when it comes to veneration, the door is wide open. Like the children of Israel in Jesus' time, much of the body of Christ is failing to discern the difference between veneration and idolatry. So let's gain clarity by examining the vocabulary.

Veneration is "respect or awe inspired by the dignity, wisdom, dedication, or talent of a person."[1] It is also "the act of venerating" an "icon, a relic," and so on.[2] *Idolatry* is defined as "the worship of a physical object as a god…[the] immoderate attachment or devotion to something."[3] The words seem similar, but each has its own emphasis. *Veneration* focuses on admiration. *Idolatry* focuses on adoration. You can admire someone for their achievements, or you can worship the ground someone walks on. The first can be compared with fanaticism toward athletes, for example. The second is more like adoring a cult leader you see as being godlike. There's nothing wrong with admiring a sports figure, but it becomes unhealthy when you start trying to emulate that individual.

Veneration is not always bad, but it can lead to an unhealthy view of someone or something. Idolatry is always bad.

Consider the ark of the covenant in the Old Testament. God conveyed His "commands to the people of Israel" by talking to Moses "from above the atonement cover between the gold cherubim" (Exod. 25:22). During the Israelites' travels, only Levites carried the ark. I believe the people appropriately valued the ark but over time came to view it as some kind of magic trinket they could pull out on the battlefield whenever they needed it, as I believe the following passage shows. It takes place after the Philistines won a battle against Israel.

> So they [the people] sent men to Shiloh to bring the Ark of the Covenant of the LORD of Heaven's Armies, who is enthroned between the cherubim. Hophni and Phinehas, the sons of Eli, were also there with the Ark of the Covenant of God. When all the Israelites saw the Ark of the Covenant of the LORD coming into the camp, their shout of joy was so loud it made the ground shake!
>
> —1 SAMUEL 4:4–5

The children of Israel assumed that venerating the ark would cause God's presence to serve as their good luck charm. Unfortunately, however, they lost the battle. The ark was captured and remained missing for some twenty years. Their veneration did not stop the Philistines from defeating them because their trust was misplaced. The power wasn't in the ark but in the One the ark represents—God.

Many people venerate man-made or self-imposed rules and assume God's presence has to dwell on such rules, but they find themselves defeated all the time because God is not obligated to bless what He has not sanctioned nor empower what He has not stipulated.

Judah's King Hezekiah addressed a similar situation when God's people idolized the bronze serpent Moses fashioned during the wilderness journey. Hezekiah saw the people's behavior as a stumbling block, and he destroyed the article.

> Hezekiah did what was pleasing in the LORD's sight, just as his ancestor David had done. He removed the pagan shrines, smashed the sacred pillars, and cut down the Asherah poles. He broke up the bronze serpent that Moses had made, because the people of Israel had been offering sacrifices to it. The bronze serpent was called Nehushtan.
> —2 KINGS 18:3–4

Idolatry caused the children of Israel to worship something God once used to heal His people. Idolatry can bring swifter punishment than veneration. Scripture condemns idolatry and has a lot to say about it; it has little to say about veneration, however. This and the fact that many believers fail to discern the line between appropriate honor and improper veneration can make veneration an easy temptation for the kingdom of darkness to use.

VENERATION AND LEAVEN

In our day, veneration begins with teachings that shape narratives and worldviews. Once lessons take root in your mind, they shape your attitudes, actions, and allegiances. An unscrupulous teacher can gain your allegiance and turn you into a zealot (disciple). The teacher's influence can remain long after the teacher is gone. With an analogy everyone could grasp, Jesus warned about this very thing:

> "Watch out!" Jesus warned them. "Beware of the yeast [leaven] of the Pharisees and Sadducees."...Then at last they understood

that he wasn't speaking about the yeast in bread, but about the deceptive teaching of the Pharisees and Sadducees.

—MATTHEW 16:6, 12

The leaven, or *yeast*, Jesus mentioned was the teachings of the Pharisees and Sadducees. The analogy was powerful because everyone understood how a little leaven goes a long way. Once the baker adds yeast to the dough, it dominates the whole lump. The baker is the teacher; the dough is the disciple, and the teaching is the leaven, which the disciple absorbs. In this context leaven is potentially dangerous.

This is why the children of Israel continued to see themselves as Moses's disciples despite the Messiah's arrival. For them and for us, breaking away from legalism is as hard as removing the leaven from dough that is already mixed. The dough never dominates the leaven; the leaven always overtakes the dough.

Besides the leaven, another factor—a supernatural connection—fueled Israel's veneration for Moses. He wasn't only an important figurehead in Israel; he was interwoven into the fabric of society. The same is true of legalism. It's woven so tightly into the fabric of the person and community that nobody can see beyond it.

I now understand why my wife and I have argued over this issue—sometimes for hours! She was raised in seriously legalistic churches and constantly told me, "Alex, it's all they know. You can't get mad at people for being ignorant when legalism is all they see."

Ibelize's statement is so accurate. Imagine telling the children of Israel, a people who were groomed and raised with the Law of Moses, that they should abandon what they knew and follow a new system built on grace. Such an idea would naturally freak them out! Moses delivered the children of Israel from Pharaoh and four centuries of slavery. Add to that the miracles, signs, and wonders they saw under Moses's leadership. These experiences created an emotional bond to Moses. The people were grateful to him and had the utmost respect and admiration for him. Moses therefore became a national figure whose name and reputation never faded.

However, the people's feelings eventually devolved into unhealthy veneration. They became such dutiful disciples of Moses that they seemed to forget what he told them in Deuteronomy 18:15: "The LORD your God will raise up for you a prophet like me from among your fellow Israelites. You must listen to him."

Instead of looking ahead to the Messiah, Israel cherished Moses's domination of their lives. It's no wonder Jesus had such a hard time reaching them. Even the early church (those who accepted Christ's sacrifice) struggled with legalism! For example, in Acts 11:1–3 Jewish believers criticized Peter for dining in a Gentile's home. And remember the report in Acts 15 of Judaizers who wanted new converts to keep the law and be circumcised (see the introduction of this book).

Zeal is part of legalism, as we will soon see. But it is already clear that the early church found it hard to transition out of the old system (the Law of Moses). Because the leaven had "permeated every part of the dough" (Luke 13:21), the Jews became zealots for the law. Therefore, leaving the legalistic system would require their detoxification. But that would require understanding the leavening process.

How leaven works

Remember: A little leaven goes a long way, and once it's added to the dough, it permeates the entire lump. Luke 13:21 speaks of three measures of dough being permeated. Because it is a parable, I see this as indicating the (following) three ways in which people who are leavened become acolytes:

1. By a person (a visionary and teacher)

2. By a teaching (the vision and teaching itself)

3. Through water baptism (submission to the vision and teaching)

In Jesus' day, becoming someone's disciple wasn't like following your favorite athlete today. Discipleship meant total surrender to the vision and teaching of the teacher (usually a rabbi), who became your master. In essence, you became an extension of your master. Jesus talked about the disciple being "as his master, and the servant as his lord" (Matt. 10:25, KJV). He added, "If they have called the master of the house Beelzebub, how much more shall they call them of his household?" (Matt. 10:25, KJV). Culturally, the idea of a teacher-master was widely understood.

Christians today can become as devoted to legalism as the Jews became to their master, Moses. But let's be fair. Many people have been rescued from the depths of sin and brought to faith in Christ through legalistic church systems. God has used these systems to help people, and many are eternally grateful. Over time, however, instead of abiding deeper in Christ, many become acolytes of legalism. Thus, the teaching of Jesus is replaced by a Law-of-Moses form of Christianity, which can propagate a mean-spirited faith detached from Christ.

The person of Moses
Once the children of Israel understood Moses was God's handpicked deliverer, every Israelite's goal was to be like Moses. The Book of Hebrews attests that "Moses was certainly faithful in God's house as a servant. His work was an illustration of the truths God would reveal later" (3:5).

The concept of faithfulness is captured in one word: *consistency*. Moses was Israel's consistent, ever-present reminder to return to God and follow His laws. This is also where contemporary legalism starts. From legalistic pulpits every week, the faithful are reminded to pursue God through a list of dos and don'ts. Many sermons focus on Moses's face-to-face conversations with God and encourage parishioners to pursue the Lord with the same intensity Moses did.

Here is the problem: The person of Jesus Christ and the idea of abiding in Him are inadvertently replaced; instead of revering Jesus, these Christians look to Moses. Being like Moses seems to them an admirable goal; but the New Testament calls all Christians to be like Christ. Patterning our lives around a Mosaic worldview is error.

Early in my ministry walk (circa 1998), I began preaching more frequently at my local church. Many of my sermons revolved around the fire of God and the shekinah glory. I didn't realize I was pushing a Moses-tabernacle-centered message, but I knew we really had church! Then when I started preaching more Christ-centered messages, the people's reactions were lackluster, as though messages about Jesus were for baby Christians, but messages on the fire of God were for the mature. You might be thinking the situation couldn't possibly have been that cultish. But it was!

The bottom line is clear: Your first step in acknowledging the person who is to become your teacher-master is to discern whether their mandate is from God. This is critical because you will begin to emulate your teacher's likes and dislikes, strengths, vocabulary, and mannerisms. Vet the person before you follow.

The teaching of Moses

Moses and Israel were bound together in a master-and-disciples relationship based on God's calling of Moses and His commitment to liberate Israel. Becoming a disciple means acknowledging the importance of teaching. Without it there can be no students. From Israel's perspective the law controlled every aspect of life. (More than 613 laws were either given to Moses by God or created by Moses to govern the Israelites' behavior.)

From the perspective of contemporary legalism, doctrines form the core. The apostle Paul wrote about sound doctrine, but in modern legalistic systems sound doctrine refers to dogmas or bylaws. These become *the* law of the land: They govern everything the church does, and everyone must obey them, just as surely as Moses commanded the Israelites to obey the Ten Commandments.

Jesus expected His disciples to follow His teachings, which were 100 percent sound:

> Why do you keep calling me "Lord, Lord!" when you don't do what I say? I will show you what it's like when someone comes to me, listens to my teaching, and then follows it. It is like a person building a house who digs deep and lays the foundation on solid rock. When the floodwaters rise and break against that house, it stands firm because it is well built. But anyone who hears and doesn't obey is like a person who builds a house right on the ground, without a foundation. When the floods sweep down against that house, it will collapse into a heap of ruins.
>
> —LUKE 6:46–49

Legalistic churches expect their members to observe the bylaws without question, and any disobedience is met with swift consequences. (The question is whether their doctrine is as sound as they believe it to be.) Like with the children of Israel, who were fearful when they received the law at Mount Sinai, fear is very present in today's legalistic churches.

The baptism of Moses

Becoming a disciple involves the outward sign of water baptism. This is a well-known sacrament in the church, but the rite was also common for followers of John the Baptist and the Pharisees. In type and shadow the Israelites who crossed the Red Sea "were baptized as followers of Moses" (1 Cor. 10:2). In this way, Israel declared to the then-known world that Moses was their rabbi. Water sealed the deal for them, as it does for today's followers of Christ.

The celebratory act of baptism provides a strong emotional connection to the teacher. As if to prove the strength of Moses's influence on the Israelites, the law was called the Law of Moses. Moses was a national figure who took the people's disobedience so personally that the Lord had to remind Moses who the people were really disobeying! "The LORD asked Moses, 'How long will these people refuse to obey *my* commands and instructions?'" (Exod. 16:28, emphasis added).

The bond that is reinforced by baptism in legalistic churches makes it harder for them to be moved by the "foreign" message of grace. Combined with the person and the teaching, baptism helps us understand how legalism becomes so deeply entrenched. That does not mean Christ isn't involved in legalistic churches. He is present; however, He is often relegated to a back seat.

Personally, I wish I hadn't spent the first half of the past thirty years in legalism. But God knew my heart and eventually drew me out. I hope the cords of His grace will open your eyes and pull you out, even as you read this book. You might struggle with concepts that seem new to you. But if you press in by faith, you will stand fast in the liberty with which Christ has made you free!

Human Idolatry

We have already examined doctrinal idolatry, but idolatry takes many shapes, and human idolatry is common in legalistic systems. The apostle John addressed this issue when he wrote, "Children, keep yourselves from idols" (1 John 5:21, KJV). John was talking not about statues but about our human devotion to anything other than God that ends up governing how we live. For example, you can idolize your church, your pastor, your denomination, or even your way of interpreting Scripture. You can even idolize the rules, regulations, and bylaws of your church.

The children of Israel were rightly devoted to Moses's teaching. He was the human vessel God appointed to deliver them from slavery, after all. He also served as their pastor and leader and was deeply involved in their lives overall. Therefore, the children of Israel were prepared to do anything for Moses.

Without realizing it, over the centuries, the people began to filter their relationship with God through the lens of Moses, to the point of being so blinded that they couldn't embrace Jesus. The Law of Moses became a veil over their understanding. Consider what Paul wrote to the church at Corinth:

> We are not like Moses, who put a veil over his face so the people of Israel would not see the glory, even though it was destined to fade away. But the people's minds were hardened, and to this day whenever the old covenant is being read, the same veil covers their minds so they cannot understand the truth. And this veil can be removed only by believing in Christ.
> —2 Corinthians 3:13–14

As you can see from this passage, Moses's teachings blinded the Jews of Jesus' day and kept them from receiving the truth of the gospel. The people did not worship him in my opinion. However, they certainly came to venerate him, as the Jewish leaders' resistance to Jesus clearly demonstrated. Their doctrinal idolatry was also evident at the time of Christ. They were so stuck on the letter of the law that they resisted Jesus' teaching on the intent of the law. Some of the most confrontational moments during Jesus' earthly ministry came when He challenged the legalistic system, as we will see.

Legalism: A False Gospel and Doctrine of Demons

The title of this section is a tip-off: I have zero tolerance for the legalistic doctrine, culture, and worldview that attempts to appease God through human effort. I love the people manipulated by legalism, but I reject any connection between legalism and true biblical holiness. Legalism is a false gospel, and demons love it. So yes, I am righteously indignant, knowing firsthand how this kind of religious spirit brainwashes God's people.

Brainwashing is "any method of controlled systematic indoctrination, [especially] one based on repetition or confusion."[4] Unfortunately, many fanatical, cultlike church movements and outright cults use repetition, confusion, and other means to force people to change their beliefs. This process is, in my opinion, more about proselytizing or propagandizing than it is about evangelizing. The methods can range from mild to severe, but it's still brainwashing, and it can begin in new members' classes. The classes aren't the problem; the intent is. Manipulating or forcing people to adhere to harsh or unbiblical tenets is demonic.

The moment you embrace the leaven in a legalistic church, you enter into dogmatism. *Dogmatism* is "a theory of cognition and personality" that focuses on "the organization and structure of both belief and disbelief systems rather than upon their content."[5] Let's be honest: For the sake of the organization, a certain amount of dogma exists in every church. Therefore, I won't single out legalistic Charismatic churches. Other denominations and many fundamentalist churches can be equally dogmatic. Dogmatism is evident when church members or leaders are extremely proud or vocal about their movement or stream of Christianity. This strong devotion comes with a tendency to (1) be critical, (2) downplay the message of the cross, and (3) make secondary doctrines primary.

If you're thinking, "Yup, that's me. I'm dogmatic," your dogma might be off or outdated. Or perhaps what you were taught is incomplete. In Acts 22:3–4 the apostle Paul talked about how his zeal made it seem right to persecute Christians. If Paul confessed his wrong dogma, I think we can do the same. Let's make sure we're not acting the way Paul did before his Damascus road encounter with Christ. Let's not fight Jesus by fighting against members in His body. (See Acts 9:4–5.)

Symptoms of the Leaven of Legalism

Many ungodly symptoms or manifestations result from bad leaven. Let's focus on three of them:

1. Double-mindedness
2. Judgmental attitudes
3. Elitism

Double-mindedness

You might never have connected legalism with double-mindedness, but those who grew up in legalistic churches can testify to the link. We know what the Bible says: "A double minded man is unstable in all his ways" (Jas. 1:8, KJV). But why are legalistic people prone to being double-minded? I believe it is because of the battle being waged within them—a struggle between what the Bible says and what the church or pastor approves or teaches. Add to that the power of groupthink to control individuals and condemn those who don't conform. The task of gaining acceptance by complying with rules and regulations consumes a lot of brainpower and emotional energy. After years of living this way, mental fractures occur, and double-mindedness increases.

No matter how obedient you are in a legalistic setting, it is never enough. This makes people miserable and unable to make choices without second-guessing themselves. Legalism causes people to doubt and become unstable, "like a wave of the sea that is driven and tossed by the wind" (Jas. 1:6, ESV). This is not a formula for well-being.

Judgmental attitudes

When you are leavened by Moses and not Jesus, being judgmental becomes a way of life. The gospel becomes unnecessarily complicated, with bylaws and other man-made rules robbing you of the simplicity of living in Christ. Instead of being a godly lover of the church, you become a hard critic, weighed down by unbiblical burdens, and no fun to be around. Judgmental attitudes keep you enforcing the rules instead of bringing people to the cross of Jesus Christ.

Paul traced legalism's beguiling and corrupting aspects all the way back to the Garden of Eden, writing, "I fear, lest by any means, as the serpent beguiled Eve through his subtilty, so your minds should be corrupted from the simplicity that is in Christ" (2 Cor. 11:3, KJV).

Elitism

Elitism is relational poison. The elitist ostracizes those people (including Christians) who have a different point of view. Elitists see themselves as arbiters of truth, and many even say nobody else has the truth that they have. This sounds cultlike by modern standards, but Jesus and His disciples also encountered elitism. Jesus' perspective might surprise you:

> John said to Jesus, "Teacher, we saw someone using your name to cast out demons, but we told him to stop because he wasn't in our group." "Don't stop him!" Jesus said. "No one who performs a miracle in my name will soon be able to speak evil of me. Anyone who is not against us is for us."
> —Mark 9:38–40

John's reaction was elitist. Jesus taught him well, but John gave himself to religion and adopted an us-and-them mentality. So Jesus corrected him. How I wish those entangled in legalism would honor this truth: "There are many parts, but only one body" (1 Cor. 12:20). There is only one body of Christ.

JUDGMENTALISM AND ELITISM IN ACTION

The things that happened in Jesus' day still happen today. The fall of man remains evident in modern attitudes and organizations. Let's survey two contemporary examples.

Westboro Baptist Church and judgmentalism

This church has been in the news for years. Westboro Baptist is infamous for their harsh criticism and judgmentalism, and they are widely hated as a result. The church's members take constitutional freedom of speech very seriously and often push the envelope as they publicly confront groups with whom they strongly disagree.

Westboro's members have picketed with signs that say, "Thank God for AIDS," and, "God is your enemy."[6] Scripture calls us to "walk in love" (Eph. 5:2, ESV), but the leaven of religion has produced ugly, judgmental attitudes in Westboro's congregation. I am sure they genuinely feel they are doing the right thing. But wrong teaching and bad theology can distort a person's or congregation's worldview and cause them to rationalize the terrible actions they choose.

Righteous judgment and judgmentalism are not the same thing. The Bible tells us to judge in a correct manner and "not according to the appearance" (John 7:24, KJV). Westboro seems to have deleted this command from its worldview. If you are from this church, I appeal to you. I know that you love God in your unique way, but your attempts to please Him are unscriptural. I sincerely pray you would continue to read this book with an open heart. May you speak "the truth in love" and "grow up into him in all things" (Eph. 4:15, KJV).

Los Rabakukus and elitism

The Rabakukus are a small Pentecostal sect in the Dominican Republic. Rabakuku is not the church's official name, but they have taken social media by storm within the Latino hyper-Pentecostal churches. They are known for their hyperlegalism, extreme dress code, aggressive preaching style, way of speaking in tongues, and immense hostility toward church organizations that don't follow their supposed *sana doctrina* (sound doctrine).

The Rabakukus achieved online notoriety during the COVID-19 pandemic. Since then many of these churches have demonstrated an extreme elitism, believing they are the only ones who still hold to sound doctrine. The leaven of religion is evident in their conduct. Their preaching and teaching videos do not offer encouragement but only offer correction. They appointed themselves as watchers over the Latino Pentecostal churches, and instead of being a blessing to the body of Christ, they have been largely banished from fellowship with Hispanic Pentecostals.

For anyone who brings biblical correction to the group, the Rabakukus meet them with fierce hostility and public ridicule.

This is classic cultlike behavior, and many young Latinos from the Dominican Republic are falling victim to it. As younger people embrace the group and emulate its founder, they become even more extreme than their predecessors.

Over time, various pastors have broken away from the group's extremes; but they have failed to remove the leaven of religiosity and still embrace a milder form of elitism. Whether the group is saved or not is not my call. But they are certainly very religious. As a Latino coming out of Hispanic legalism, it is my prayer that this group would read this book and abandon legalism.

If you are part of the Rabakukus, I neither judge nor reject you. But I invite you to reconsider your estimations of sound doctrine in the light of Scripture rather than man-made traditions. Let the Holy Spirit show you how to honor God in your lifestyle, as you read the following passage again:

> You have died with Christ, and he has set you free from the spiritual powers of this world. So why do you keep on following the rules of the world, such as, "Don't handle! Don't taste! Don't touch!"? Such rules are mere human teachings about things that deteriorate as we use them. These rules may seem wise because they require strong devotion, pious self-denial, and severe bodily discipline. But they provide no help in conquering a person's evil desires.
> —COLOSSIANS 2:20–23

BREAKING FREE AND MOVING FORWARD

No matter how long you've been in a legalistic system, you can unlearn what you've been taught. The Holy Spirit is powerful enough to draw you out with truth and cause you to embrace a new system of sound doctrine. Just remain willing to follow His leading.

Detoxify

Freeing yourself from legalism begins with changes in your spiritual diet. This takes time, so don't rush it. A hasty shift away from a Mosaic mindset can leave you more vulnerable to the pressures, peer attacks, and feelings of false guilt that crop up as you extricate yourself from the system. Being manipulated by legalism was a process. Detoxing is a process too.

In the physical sense, detoxification removes harmful elements from your body. Detoxing from legalism means purging the system's doctrines and environment from your life. At times, it will require you to purge the brethren as well. The leaven of legalism slowly stifles and frustrates your walk with Christ. The brainwashing grooms you, but recovery is available. The key is to detach yourself from anything legalistic.

When I was a young ordained evangelist in the legalistic churches, I attended a hyperlegalistic revival service. That night, the preacher went hard against worldliness. I found myself impressed by his passion and by the crowd's intense reaction. So I decided to imitate his style. When I got no reaction from the crowd, I asked the Lord what was wrong. He said, "I did not call you to preach that message. I want you to take the sermon you are preparing and black out every part of it connected to legalistic thinking."

After fifteen minutes of reviewing my message, I'd crossed out at least 75 percent of it. I sensed the Lord saying, "I want you to preach what's not crossed out." When I did that, almost half of the church came to the altar, crying out to God and experiencing revival. Immediately, I felt the Lord telling me this was the way He wanted me to preach.

I protested and said, "I don't know how to preach like this."

I'm telling you this because after that experience, I had to detox myself! Once I stopped operating under the leaven of Moses, it took me months and even years to develop my approach and relearn everything I knew about writing sermons.

Transitioning from the Moses model to the Jesus model takes

effort, but it's worth it! It's about Jesus, not Moses, and the sooner you make the change, the sooner you will get free. Purging the old leaven and replacing it is more than mental modification; it is heart transformation. The following passage from Leviticus presents the detox process in type and shadow, so notice the details.

> Next Moses took the fat, the fat tail…the internal organs, the long lobe of the liver, and the two kidneys and the fat around them, along with the right thigh. On top of these he placed a thin cake of bread made without yeast, a cake of bread mixed with olive oil, and a wafer spread with olive oil. All these were taken from the basket of bread made without yeast that was placed in the LORD's presence. He put all these in the hands of Aaron and his sons, and he lifted these gifts as a special offering to the LORD. Moses then took all the offerings back from them and burned them on the altar on top of the burnt offering. This was the ordination offering. It was a pleasing aroma, a special gift presented to the LORD.
> —LEVITICUS 8:25–28

Notice Moses was required to remove the fat from the offering. Legalism is the fat that mars your worship to God. Consider any teachings from an old wineskin as fat—views and concepts that are foreign to the gospel of Christ. It is added stuff, and it's another gospel altogether. (See Galatians 1:6–7.)

Do what the apostle Paul did: Take everything you learned from the past and place it before your great High Priest, Jesus. Then ask Him to change it. When I cried out daily for God to help me trade the leaven of legalism for a Christ-centered and cross-focused theology, He challenged me to reevaluate my dogmatic views. I had to cut out the fat (the tenets of my denomination).

Until you cut the fat from your theology, your teaching and preaching will dishonor Christ, and any praise you receive will come from people rather than God. Just as Moses burned the fat he removed from his sacrifice, you need to burn up your old views and allow God to upgrade your spiritual programming (like He did when He told me to detox my sermon).

Cutting away the fat isn't easy, but as Paul said, "Everything else is worthless when compared with the infinite value of knowing Christ Jesus my Lord. For his sake I have discarded everything else, counting it all as garbage, so that I could gain Christ" (Phil. 3:8).

Until you are just as determined to do whatever it takes to detox, you are not ready for what's next. It took Paul fourteen years to detox from his Mosaic mindset. (See Galatians 2:1–2.) I doubt it will take you fourteen years to break free of legalism, but be patient and don't fake it! Allow the gospel of grace to leaven your new batch of dough, and allow the Holy Spirit to retrain you. You will not regret it.

Deny yourself and take up the cross

The next step in turning away from the leaven of Moses involves doing what Jesus told His disciples to do. He said, "If any man will come after me, let him deny himself, and take up his cross, and follow me" (Matt. 16:24, KJV).

This statement might sound elementary, but it's essential. The leaven of religion never tells you to deny yourself. Why? Because, at its root, legalism is selfish. It's centered on what you can accomplish, and it detracts from the efficacy of Christ's work on the cross.

Jesus said to deny yourself and carry the cross. Legalism says to deny your flesh and take up the rules. Denying yourself is not a denial *of* self. Denying yourself means denying *something*. Your breakthrough is not about what you do but about what you carry—not the rules but your cross! This means letting go of the traditions of men. The cross is heavy, and the rules are heavy. You cannot carry both. So become preoccupied with obeying Jesus' command.

You reprogram yourself by carrying your cross. When was the last time you picked it up? When was the last time you denied yourself—your passions, desires, and preconceived ideas? Legalism constricts people to a rigorous set of rules that leads to self-denial but not a denial of self. They don't remove the desire; they only regulate the behavior, as Colossians 2:23 says: "These rules may seem wise because they require strong devotion, pious self-denial, and severe bodily discipline. But they provide no help in conquering a person's evil desires."

When you take up your cross, your only preoccupation is to follow Jesus. Matthew 16:24 does not say to follow Moses or Elijah (like the modern prophetic movement tends to do), or Enoch, Noah, or Daniel. You're not even called to follow King David. You are to follow Jesus, "the author and finisher of [your] faith; who for the joy that was set before him endured the cross, despising the shame, and is set down at the right hand of the throne of God" (Heb. 12:2, KJV).

Jesus will lead you on paths you might not choose, but they'll place you exactly where you need to be—no longer in control or trying to prove what you can do for God. No. You will simply follow Him and discover all that He has done for you. Jesus talked to Peter about being led. He said,

> I tell you the truth, when you were young, you were able to do as you liked; you dressed yourself and went wherever you wanted to go. But when you are old, you will stretch out your hands, and others will dress you and take you where you don't want to go.
>
> —JOHN 21:18

Now take a moment and pray this prayer:

> *Jesus, please lead me by Your Spirit. Show me where and how I have focused on Moses or some other figure rather than on You. Reveal to me how I preached or listened to sermons in ways that did not see You at the very center. Remind me of the legalistic things I have said about "old-time religion" or being "kept in line" by rules, manipulation, or punishment. Please show me my own legalistic ways, and guide me into the riches of Your grace. I pray this in Jesus' name. Amen.*

Yes! You can detox from a works-based gospel. Let Paul's words settle deep in your heart: "Purge out therefore the old leaven, that ye may be a new lump, as ye are unleavened. For even Christ our passover is sacrificed for us" (1 Cor. 5:7, KJV).

So be it, until all that is left is the leaven of Christ!

Chapter 3

FEAR-BASED OBEDIENCE

Then Saul admitted to Samuel, "Yes, I have sinned. I have disobeyed your instructions and the LORD's command, for I was afraid of the people and did what they demanded."
—1 SAMUEL 15:24

FEAR IS A mighty manipulator. When unchecked, it sparks confusion, blame shifting, strife, and an unquestioned devotion to rules. Fear takes your eye off the ball while prodding you to care about unimportant things you then try to control. Legalism thrives on fear and requires fear-based obedience that is both misdirected and exhausting.

Some of the biggest arguments my wife and I had back in the day involved something I thought was almost silly: the way our church and denomination cared so much about other believers' opinions and words. I had little interest in the matter, but my wife reminded me, "These are God's people. You must care."

My rebuttal was always the same: "Well, God's people can be wrong."

When I got really mad, I would yell, "I don't care what Christians think because I'm not scared of church people."

Now, after twenty years in the pastorate and some maturing of my views, I can honestly see a difference between respecting one another's views (which the Bible commands us to do) and allowing church consensus to control what God wants to do or say (as if we ever could).

Obviously, tolerance is crucial to living in the unity Jesus prayed for in John 17. So Paul commanded us to be respectful, writing, "One person esteems one day as better than another, while another esteems all days alike. Each one should be fully convinced in his own mind" (Rom. 14:5, ESV). Paul is saying that forcing your personal convictions on believers is unbiblical and divisive.

The question is, What happens when personal convictions and matters of conscience hinder individual discipleship or the church's advancement? Take, for example, the old dogmatic view that women cannot wear pants in the church, or even the modified version that says women can wear pants in the church, except on the altar or when preaching. Both ideas are religious and difficult to reform, not because the enforcers necessarily believe them but because they are afraid of how people might respond if the dogma is changed.

Fear always exacts a price. In the women's slacks example, the enforcers could have been catalysts of change. Instead, they succumbed to groupthink. Your church or denomination might be one where this issue arises. Truth be told, you probably don't care much about rules for ladies' slacks because you know in your heart that God is not sending women to hell for their attire. However, if you're a woman, you probably keep wearing skirts to church. You've thought about mustering the strength to wear respectable pants to church, but you keep backing out. My question is, *Why?*

Let me first lay down a disclaimer: I am not picking on what women wear to church or what some people think they should or shouldn't wear to church. It just so happens that the lingering issue of women in pants is a perfect example of the dynamics surrounding legalism, and fear is among them.

COERCION IN THE CHURCH

Why is it so difficult to reform the dogma that stifles churches? The cause, in my opinion, is coercion. When people who obey rules like the ones involving women's attire in church are asked whether they are being coerced by man-made rules, they almost always say no. But they are being coerced. Speaking from my experience as pastor of a church, I was made to enforce certain rules in order to keep peace in the church. Even as the pastor I was coerced.

If you disagree with an article in your church's dogma, but you obey it to keep the peace, you are being coerced. *Coercion* is "the act or process of persuading someone forcefully to do something that they do not want to do…[coercion is the] force or the power to use force in gaining compliance, as by a government or police force."[1] So compliance is the goal of coercion. *Compliance* is not an inherently bad word, but it is overemphasized in some church contexts. So how many times have you heard that word in a church meeting? And why have you heard it?

Coercion is not always overt; but even if it isn't, reformation doesn't come easily in the church setting. And when coercion works in reverse, church leaders seem to worship at the feet of those who serve and attend their churches. Pastors are caught in the undercurrent of coercion, just like everyone else. Many senior pastors I have met don't believe in their own churches' dogmas. Yet because their denominations placed them in leadership, they try not to ruffle feathers.

You can rest assured that the slightest hint of change will cause someone to complain. Even when God seems to author the change, it ends up being disallowed and disapproved. Pastors become like Manchurian candidates, puppets manipulated by the members' opinions. That is coercion, and it's costly. When fear of the people prevents leaders and churches from reforming church culture, what's left is not reformation but refrigeration and the reheating of old dogmas.

The Makings of Passive Leaders

Why is the resistance to change so fierce? Personally, I don't believe God's called leaders consciously decide to become passive. I think the people's resistance to change contributes to leaders' lack of stamina and passion to bring much-needed change. They develop an unhealthy fear of the people, and the following are four big reasons why.

1. Conscience
2. Fear of man
3. Opinions
4. Groupthink (more on this soon)

These four reasons are prevalent in legalistic church environments. Unless churches address them, the fear of church people will continue to dominate church culture, and legalism will continue to cause stagnation—not only in churches but in the lives of their congregants. So let's take a closer look at how each element works.

Slaves to someone else's conscience

Whether we are pastors or church members, the first element we need to overcome is the enslavement to other people's consciences. Yes, we need to respect other people's convictions. But let's also acknowledge that some people refuse to change. Respect for other people's convictions can easily be used to manipulate God's people, prevent change, and hold entire congregations captive to the preferences of a few—including preferences that are absurd and unbiblical.

The following absurd conviction has been circulating all over social media: A beloved pastor said if you drink coffee, you are taking cocaine. Therefore, drinking coffee makes you a drug addict. I'm not judging this pastor, but his statement is scientifically incorrect. Caffeine is not cocaine, and convictions like this must be refuted. To believe that we should honor such a baseless conviction is insanity. We absolutely should not!

My opinion might seem harsh. And I confess that multiple texts in the Epistles tell us to respect the consciences of other believers. But the Scriptures don't say that we cannot refute them. Respecting and refuting are not mutually exclusive concepts. And respecting other people's consciences goes both ways. Paul said, "You must be careful so that your freedom does not cause others with a weaker conscience to stumble" (1 Cor. 8:9). Paul's statement is true, but it is not meant to give our legalistic brethren a pass for their stifling rules. The legalistic person must also consider whether they are violating the convictions of others. The pastor who likened coffee drinkers to drug addicts needs to ask himself how many believers have stumbled because of what he said.

My wife, Ibelize, can remember more stories of absurd personal convictions than most people can imagine. She witnessed these stories during her long history in legalistic churches. Many of the convictions upheld were clearly unbiblical, and I often asked her why no one ever challenged them. Her reply was always the same: "We were taught to respect people's convictions."

All I could say was, "But this conviction isn't biblical."

Then my wife would look at me, shrug her shoulders, and walk away.

The issue of conscience is important. One person can start a holy war based on a personal conviction. When my first church (He Is Risen Tabernacle) embraced Christian hip-hop and began allowing young people to host gospel rap concerts at church to evangelize their friends, we faced strong backlash, and pastors banned their church members from fellowshipping at our church. One day, an older sister so disagreed with rap music in the church that she said she "saw demons coming out of the church speakers"!

Yes, that is exactly what she said. That was not God speaking; it was her personal conviction, her conscience, and the fact that she did not value Christian rap music. It was an attempt to control others. Let me say, however, that during those years, our church won many young people to Christ who still attend our church and serve the Lord. Also, many churches reached out and asked us how they could use Christian rap in their evangelism. The interest and desire were there, but many churches dropped the transition because an influential person or group was bothered by hip-hop and couldn't see God redeeming it for His purposes.

We must willingly challenge people who hold convictions based more on culture or opinion than on the Word. If we don't lovingly ask why their consciences are bothered by things that aren't sin, we risk bringing confusion or shipwreck to the faith of many. As Paul told Timothy, "Cling to your faith in Christ, and keep your conscience clear. For some people have deliberately violated their consciences; as a result, their faith has been shipwrecked" (1 Tim. 1:19).

Especially if you are a pastor or leader, ask yourself the following questions:

» Are these convictions truly biblical?

» Are individuals' convictions hindering the progress of this church?

» Do I need to challenge this misuse of Scripture in regard to conscience?

Fear of man

Now, let's address a battle every believer faces to some degree: the fear of man. To overcome legalism, we *must* reject this fear. This is especially important for those struggling to exit or reform a legalistic system.

The fear of man brings a snare, and snares bring consequences. Proverbs 29:25 says, "Fear of man will prove to be a snare, but whoever trusts in the LORD is kept safe" (NIV). The Hebrew word translated "snare" in this verse describes what happens when a hunter sets a trap: The snares don't kill the prey; the snares immobilize and debilitate them. It's a painful place for an animal to be.

Years ago, God impressed me to bring change to various departments of the church. I became fearful and second-guessed whether I was hearing from God. Looking back, I believe I justified my failure to bring change. The truth is that I hesitated because I feared the people. I was new to the pastorate and thought our biggest givers would leave the church. I was afraid those who disagreed with change would stir up gossip and undermine the church. It hurts to share this, but I must because you might be a pastor who is dealing with this issue right now!

The fear of man contaminates good judgment. It produces decisions that aren't in God's heart and won't serve the best interests of the ministry. Fear causes you to show partiality by giving the most honor to the biggest gossipers in the church while you toss aside the people who cause no trouble, are the most faithful, and are sometimes overlooked for years.

If you fear the people, you will try resolving church matters without going to God. Why? Because you know He will remind you to obey His commands, regardless of your fears. The further you allow your fear to go, the more that intimidation will become the culture of the church. Nothing will get done because your priority will be keeping the peace. However, when Moses delegated power to other leaders, he told them, "Do not be afraid of anyone, for judgment belongs to God" (Deut. 1:17, NIV).

Becoming free of a legalistic culture requires boldness and stamina, especially when family and friends are involved. So many people remain stuck in religious contexts simply because they want to avoid all drama. My wife can tell you that I stayed in our legalistic church because, until her detox was completed years later, she was most comfortable there. We fought periodically because of my desire to leave the *sana doctrina* churches. When I finally told her I was leaving, she said (with tears in her eyes), "Alex, where am I going to go? This is all I know."

Thank God my hatred of legalism didn't land us in divorce court! My love for my wife kept me from leaving until she also wanted to be free. I wasn't the only person who wanted to leave the system. And we probably weren't the only couple who struggled with the issue. Many believers wanted to leave, but the matter was discussed privately, and nobody had the courage to actually leave.

The fear of man is not new in religious circles. During Jesus' earthly walk, people were afraid to ruffle the feathers of their Jewish leaders. "There was a lot of grumbling about [Jesus] among the crowds. Some argued, 'He's a good man,' but others said, 'He's nothing but a fraud who deceives the people.' But no one had the courage to speak favorably about him in public, for they were afraid of getting in trouble with the Jewish leaders" (John 7:12-13).

The people couldn't publicly share their thoughts on Jesus because so many Jews and Jewish leaders believed He was leading people astray. The same types of accusations were made when I embraced deliverance in our church. People accused me of leading souls away from Christ. As a result, many people who loved and respected our ministry became too afraid to join our church.

If that has happened to you, you're not alone. You may be dreaming of leaving the legalistic system, but (especially if you are involved in leadership) you fear being criticized for deserting your pastor and leaving the church with a vacant position. I had those concerns until I mustered whatever strength I had left, called a family meeting, prayed with my loved ones, and watched God lead us out!

FOPO = Fear of People's Opinions!

Recently, I reconnected with a friend from the denomination I left years ago. When my wife and I were still members, this friend was also thinking about leaving. Sadly, she couldn't get beyond the fear of people's opinions and the possible damage to her excellent reputation. So she stayed within the denomination. She has since seen God's hand in our ministry and has acknowledged it wouldn't have happened if Ibelize and I had stayed put. It saddens me to know that fifteen years after we left, this friend still feels unable to make the move.

That is what FOPO—the fear of people's opinions—does! It also causes the following:

1. Loss of confidence

2. Diminished performance

3. Burnout

4. Fear of ridicule or rejection

5. Surrendering your viewpoint when challenged

6. Playing it safe

I have seen these effects in my friend's life. Her confidence dipped. She was always tired. Her performance suffered because her heart wasn't in the church. Her husband also began to lose interest in serving. The fear of being ridiculed caused her to play it safe, and other people often stole the ideas she was afraid to raise.

Opinions can hold you captive. Yet they aren't foolproof or necessarily fact based. An *opinion* is "a view, judgment, or appraisal formed in the mind about a particular matter."[2] In Galatians chapter 2 the apostle Peter feared the opinions of others and became hypocritical because of it. Yes, even one of the Twelve was crippled by FOPO! It was enough to get Paul's attention, and he described what happened:

> When Peter came to Antioch, I had to oppose him to his face, for what he did was very wrong. When he first arrived, he ate with the Gentile believers, who were not circumcised. But afterward, when some friends of James came, Peter wouldn't eat with the Gentiles anymore. He was afraid of criticism from these people who insisted on the necessity of circumcision. As

> a result, other Jewish believers followed Peter's hypocrisy, and even Barnabas was led astray by their hypocrisy.
> —GALATIANS 2:11–13

Peter's hypocrisy was a serious concern, and even Paul's ministry companion Barnabas "was led astray." Peter's influence had already affected the established work in Galatia, so Paul confronted the issue in a public way before it overtook the fledgling church and continued spreading like a virus. Just one leader dominated by the fear of man can spread the virus to the masses—and all on the basis of an opinion!

The Bible warns us about opinions, saying, "Fools have no interest in understanding; they only want to air their own opinions" (Prov. 18:2). Don't back down because of opinions. Just know that God is watching, and in His timing, He will deal with the opinions of others.

When I left my denomination and asked them to bless my going, they reluctantly agreed. Many years later, I reconnected with my regional bishop, who told me, "Pagani, when you first left, I didn't see why you wanted to leave. But now that I see what God is doing in your life and ministry, I finally understand. And for what it's worth, you're one of my favorite internet preachers."

Wow! Those words were like honey to the embittered parts of my soul! Don't worry about people's words and opinions. In time, they will see what God is doing in your life. Stop worrying when they question your decision to leave. They might believe that God frowns on your decision, even when He is telling you to leave. So listen to Him, get up, and go!

Groupthink, excommunication, and public shaming

Legalism demands conformity, which fosters unhealthy behaviors in churches. We've talked about patterned ways of thinking that conform "to group values and ethics."[3] Among them are groupthink (which we touched on earlier), excommunication, and public shaming.

Groupthink

Groupthink makes it harder to break away from the crowd, but groupthink is not your master. Let's take a closer look at groupthink:

> Groupthink is a psychological phenomenon that occurs within a group of people in which the desire for harmony or conformity...results in an irrational or dysfunctional decision-making outcome. Cohesiveness, or the desire for cohesiveness, in a group may produce a tendency among its members to agree at all costs. This causes the group to minimize conflict and reach a consensus decision without critical evaluation.[4]

The previous definition explains why so many people have been trapped in religious environments *for years*. They're stuck in groupthink that's disguised as unity. Why? Because no one wants to be rejected or be perceived as an oddball or make the organization look bad in the world's eyes. Yet that is exactly what King Saul did when he ignored Samuel's very specific instructions. Saul was afraid of the people, so he disobeyed the Lord. Afterward, Saul wanted Samuel to keep up appearances, as though everything were OK.

> Saul said to Samuel, "I have sinned. I violated the Lord's command and your instructions. I was afraid of the men and so I gave in to them. Now I beg you, forgive my sin and come back with me, so that I may worship the Lord." But Samuel said to him, "I will not go back with you. You have rejected the word of the Lord, and the Lord has rejected you as king over Israel!"
>
> —1 Samuel 15:24–26, niv

Samuel knew things weren't OK, and he refused to pretend they were. The legalistic system knows how to keep up appearances, and slaves in that system learn to do the same. They forget that people like Samuel can see through the charade. So make up your mind to reject groupthink and stop living a lie. Be like the prophet Samuel, and say no.

Excommunication

Legalism can turn a loving church into an angry mob, especially when it comes to enforcing church rules. Excommunication is an accepted custom in legalistic environments, and people are routinely excommunicated for minor violations, such as small disagreements with the pastor (especially with the pastor's wife). You can be forced to leave the church and banned from ever again talking to the person with whom you disagreed.

Disagreements in the church are supposed to be reconciled, and people are supposed to be restored. But without the fruit of the Spirit punishment is the answer, and people are cut off. The church becomes a revolving door through which some people are ejected and new people are coming in. This is not God's design for the church community.

When disagreements arise or church members mess up, resolution is the biblical answer, as Paul explained: "If another believeris overcome by some sin, you who are godlyshould gently and humbly help that person back onto the right path. And be careful not to fall into the same temptation yourself" (Gal. 6:1).

Public shaming

In a recent viral video, a young lady who became pregnant out of wedlock is forced to publicly inform the church. (As usual, the child's father is nowhere to be found.) The video instantly triggered people who grew up in churches where public shaming was the norm. The scene is no different from something that happened when Jesus taught in the temple courts: "As he was speaking, the teachers of religious law and the Pharisees brought a woman who had been caught in the act of adultery. They put her in front of the crowd" (John 8:3).

The legalistic system has no sympathy for those who violate its rules and regulations. Thank God the case of the woman in John 8 ended with Jesus forgiving her and publicly rebuking those who shamed her and requested the death penalty. Jesus' response showed shame is not the way of the kingdom!

You might be tempted to say there is nothing wrong with publicly confessing your sins to the church. Yet the Bible says, "Confess your sins to each other and pray for each other so that you may be healed. The earnest prayer of a righteous person has great power and produces wonderful results" (Jas. 5:16). This speaks of one-to-one interaction and not a group setting.

In the viral video I mentioned, the young lady apologizes to the church, and the church applauds. But no prayer is offered for her restoration. I am not defending the young lady's sin before the Lord. Nor am I saying church discipline is inherently wrong. Paul often told the church that discipline was necessary, but when discipline turns into public shaming, the leadership is not guided by Scripture; it's responding to a personal vendetta.

If your church shamed you, whether recently or long ago, I believe God wants to heal your church hurt and cause the latter part of your story to be greater than the former part. God did not tell anyone to publicly shame you. The Bible says quite the opposite: "Above all, love each other deeply, because love covers over a multitude of sins" (1 Pet. 4:8, NIV). This is true, no matter what you did. The blood of Jesus Christ covered it. Now go and sin no more!

The days of allowing the consensus to rule your life are over. If you're a pastor or leader, the days of being ruled by dogma that wasn't established with the heart of Christ are over too. No more allowing people to control you—detox from the opinions of people, and obey God with all your heart, soul, mind, and strength. Listen to what people say. Pray for them. Consider their advice. But don't let the fear of man drive you. You are no longer a people pleaser!

Breaking Free and Moving Forward

Go against the grain, biblically

The number one way to keep people from arbitrarily dictating what the Lord wants is to go against the grain, biblically. I'm not talking about rebelling against members of the church or other believers; I am saying you must become like Joshua and Caleb, who silenced the voices of those who contradicted God's ways and Word (Num. 14:6–9).

When the ten frightened spies reported to Moses, they told him about the "bountiful country…flowing with milk and honey" but added, "The people living there are powerful, and their towns are large and fortified. We even saw giants there, the descendants of Anak!" (Num. 13:27–28). In other words, they cowered and made the people of Israel afraid. "But Caleb tried to quiet the people as they stood before Moses. 'Let's go at once to take the land,' he said. 'We can certainly conquer it!'" (Num. 13:30).

Caleb responded quickly to shut down the unbelief that was spread by the evil report of the ten spies. When the time came, Caleb didn't allow other people's fears to stop him from conquering the land he was promised. Of course, the ten spies remained pessimistic, even after Caleb's rebuttal. Sometimes you have to stand against the negativity of your church culture, even at the expense of being seen as a rebel. But you can be like Caleb, who did not falter or surrender his faith. Many years later, God gave Caleb his own mountain! If you resist ungodly groupthink, God will reward you too.

Ignore the crowd

An important takeaway from this chapter involves Jesus' approach to handling a crowd that wanted its way: He silenced their voices in His head. When the crowd wanted Jesus to agree with stoning the woman caught in adultery, Jesus simply ignored them.

> Jesus stooped down and wrote in the dust with his finger. They kept demanding an answer, so he stood up again and said, "All right, but let the one who has never sinned throw the first stone!" Then he stooped down again and wrote in the dust. When the accusers heard this, they slipped away one by one...until only Jesus was left in the middle of the crowd with the woman. Then Jesus stood up again and said to the woman, "Where are your accusers? Didn't even one of them condemn you?"
>
> "No, Lord," she said.
>
> And Jesus said, "Neither do I. Go and sin no more."
>
> —JOHN 8:6–11

Jesus neutralized the power of groupthink and caused the crowd to focus on their own sin. This is a powerful display of wisdom and boldness because the woman was indeed caught in adultery, and the Law of Moses did command that she be stoned. But Jesus set in motion a New Covenant perspective established in grace rather than condemnation. So let God help you ignore the crowd and move forward in the grace of our Lord Jesus Christ! Let the following prayer strengthen you.

> *Lord, teach me to trust You and reject any fear of intimidation, shame, or powerlessness that once distorted my judgment. In any capacity that I am called to serve You, I ask that Your Spirit would give me the courage to lead and remain faithful to Your instruction. Grant me the stamina to stand in favor of whatever reformation You desire for Your church. And please open my lips to speak Your Word, in the name of the Father, the Son, and the Holy Spirit. Amen.*

Chapter 4

WORSHIPPING TRADITION

Who also hath made us able ministers of the new testament; not of the letter, but of the spirit: for the letter killeth, but the Spirit giveth life.
—2 Corinthians 3:6, kjv, emphasis added

THE LETTER KILLS. I like to say that legalism keeps you trapped by black letters on white pages. It's a statement I coined many years ago when I realized I was a literalist blindly following what was written, without regard to context. Driven more by the fear of going to hell than by my love for God, I was a zealot for the Scriptures. There was a context for my error: I had converted to Jesus from a prison cell and could barely believe that God would save a sinner like me. So in gratitude I decided to follow Him at all costs.

My intentions were good, but my decision was off base. God called His people not to follow His Word at all costs but to follow its proper interpretation at all costs. Our misunderstandings of the Scriptures lead to disaster. Why? Because without proper interpretation we can make scriptures say anything we want them to say—something God never intended. And we can use them to hurt and manipulate people, in His name!

Many religious wars have been fought in the name of the Bible.

Even slavery in the United States was justified by wrongly interpreted scriptures. Slave owners and others used their misperceptions to justify owning and selling human beings! That's what happens when you let those black letters on white pages rule you. You become toxic, and your Christianity becomes tainted by the demonic.

Toxic Traits

Toxicity is "the quality, state, or relative degree of being poisonous"[1]; it is "very harmful or unpleasant in a pervasive or insidious way."[2] Some poisons are deadly, even in small doses. So we must keep our theology pure. We do this by seeking the Holy Spirit for the proper understanding and interpretation of Scripture.

Poisons are so effective that one drop can contaminate a whole barrel of water. As poison, legalism and the spirit of religion and tradition work the same way. They are among the greatest hindrances to God's kingdom, which is why Jesus rebuked and corrected the Pharisees (the teachers of religious law) more than any other group. Jesus mentioned Herod once, but He addressed the Pharisees (and the Sadducees) repeatedly. He not only refuted them in public, but He offended them on purpose! The disciples even asked Him, "Do you realize you offended the Pharisees by what you just said?" (Matt. 15:12).

Today's church, which tries so hard not to offend anyone, would have a hard time with certain things Jesus said. When His disciples expressed concern about the Pharisees, Jesus responded bluntly and said, "Every plant not planted by my heavenly Father will be uprooted, so ignore them [the Pharisees]. They are blind guides leading the blind, and if one blind person guides another, they will both fall into a ditch" (Matt. 15:13–14).

Jesus said to *ignore them*! I believe He would tell us to focus on the truth and ignore today's legalistic, man-made doctrines as well. The current legalism seems so dominant because the church isn't ignoring it, and movements gain strength when they get attention.

I believe after we leave the legalistic behind, we continue practicing certain traits—and we have no idea why! Here's an example: Many legalistic Latino churches have a custom I've not seen anywhere else in Christendom. Before they read Scripture, ministers are required to say, "The Bible is read in the name of the Father, the Son, and the Holy Spirit." Obviously, honoring the Trinity is not harmful, but many who observe this practice believe that nonobservance dishonors God and the Holy Scriptures.

By creating this rule and accusing those who reject it, they've introduced a stumbling block for believers around the globe. In my experience most people who raise this accusation aren't sincerely honoring the Trinity or the Word. Perhaps without realizing it, they are using their ritual as an identity marker to let everyone else recognize their fundamental, theologically conservative views.

Whether identity is the real issue or not, rituals leave lasting impressions, even on those who leave legalistic systems. I recently visited a church whose pastors left the legalism movement more than fifteen years ago. Yet when one of them opened the Scriptures, he repeated the ritual statement I quoted above. I looked at my wife, as if to ask, "Why is he still saying that?"

What I noticed in this pastor's current church was a residue of the religious system he left behind. I suspect this is part of why his church isn't growing. Don't mistake what I'm saying here. There is nothing wrong with small churches; my point is that clinging to past religious identity markers will produce the same results it produced in the past. So beware of what you carry forward.

THE LETTER DEFINITELY KILLS

Why would I make such a prediction about what you carry forward? Because "the letter kills, but the Spirit gives life" (2 Cor. 3:6, NKJV). What a powerful statement by Paul! God gave him this revelation, perhaps because Paul (then known as *Saul*) had used the law to persecute Christians. He was so caught up in literalism that he couldn't see God's intent in what the Scriptures said.

A New Testament example is when Jesus identified Himself as the fulfillment of Scripture and said that prophets are not accepted in their hometowns. Then He added that Elijah and Elisha healed non-Jews, presumably because the prophets were not always accepted by their own people. "When they heard this, the people in the synagogue were furious. Jumping up, they mobbed him and forced him to the edge of the hill on which the town was built. They intended to push him over the cliff" (Luke 4:28–29).

Right before this outburst occurred, "everyone spoke well of [Jesus] and was amazed by the gracious words that came from his lips. 'How can this be?' they asked. 'Isn't this Joseph's son?'" (Luke 4:22).

What a dramatic shift! It was as though the people had become spiritually bipolar—inspired one moment and murderous the next! The absence of a humble posture and of revelation from the Holy Spirit positioned them this way. The letter truly kills, so much that scriptures meant to bless can instead cause people to turn on you in an instant.

The letter of the law keeps the fruit of the Spirit, the new creation, and the Word of God from being active in our lives. It kills our desire to pursue God with all our hearts, because we believe we can never measure up. The letter always finds ways to disqualify us. (I have yet to see a legalistic rule empowering anyone to live righteously.) The law is not designed to empower. It is meant to reveal our sinfulness.

Staying under the law after we have been saved by grace causes us to appease our consciences by living in unregulated zeal. This is apparent in rituals practiced by some Roman Catholics, including self-flagellation (whipping yourself until you bleed) and walking for miles on your knees to gain the justification only available through Jesus' work on the cross.

The key fact is this: Only Jesus justifies us, and it only comes by faith. As Romans 5:1–2 states, "Being justified by faith, we have peace with God through our Lord Jesus Christ: by whom also we have access by faith into this grace wherein we stand and rejoice in hope of the glory of God" (KJV). Meditate on this verse, and allow it to permeate your heart and mind. Its revolutionary truth will keep you from the fanaticism that urges you to fight your brothers and sisters in Christ.

Fanaticism always stems from wrong interpretations of Scripture. Fanatics are focused on views that blind them with darkness. But we can also be blinded by too much light.

Blinded by too much darkness

Darkness is a lack of light. Symbolically, darkness represents ignorance. Those ignorant of the Scriptures (or of their proper study) have limited understanding. This darkness results when we filter our Scripture reading through what we already know. For those who haven't attended a good Bible school or a good Bible study at church, this is a common problem. We all need to interact in the Scriptures with seasoned believers who hold us accountable for discerning the context of and rightly interpreting the Word. Yes! The Word is a lamp unto our feet and light to our path. (See Psalm 119:105.) But our own ignorance can keep us in the dark.

The apostle Paul was a model student of the great scholar Gamaliel. Yet Paul confessed to his own ignorance. He wrote, "I used to blaspheme the name of Christ. In my insolence, I persecuted his people. But God had mercy on me because I did it in ignorance and unbelief" (1 Tim. 1:13).

Sincere brothers and sisters can go astray the same way Paul did. A literal interpretation of the Word of God turned Paul against God's people. As brilliant as Paul was, he thought he was doing the right thing! Why? Because he believed that Christians were violating the Law of Moses. The letter of the law convinced Paul that killing Christians was appropriate. When Stephen was martyred, Paul (Saul) was happy to look after the coats of Stephen's accusers.

Based on Paul's beliefs at that time, I'm guessing he found a certain satisfaction in Stephen's death. Paul's spiritual blindness allowed him not to care about the murder. Later on, in Acts 13 Paul told the sorcerer Elymas, "'Watch now, for the Lord has laid his hand of punishment upon you, and you will be struck blind. You will not see the sunlight for some time.' Instantly mist and darkness came over the man's eyes, and he began groping around begging for someone to take his hand and lead him" (Acts 13:11).

Perhaps before his conversion on the road to Damascus, Paul's blindness came with such a mist because nothing could make him see until the Lord met him and opened his eyes to the light of the gospel.

Blinded by too much light

When the Lord Jesus revealed Himself to Saul of Tarsus (Paul), the man was blinded by too much light. "So his companions led him by the hand to Damascus. He remained there blind for three days and did not eat or drink" (Acts 9:8–9).

The light of Christ transformed Saul for the better. It does the same for us. But if we become prideful about our knowledge of the Word or blind to our own questionable views, too much light can have a negative effect. Have you ever talked with a know-it-all? The conversation tends to be futile because know-it-alls refuse to see any point of view but their own. Why? Because their eyes are blinded by light. Look at what the learned Paul said about himself:

> Then Paul said, "I am a Jew, born in Tarsus, a city in Cilicia, and I was brought up and educated here in Jerusalem under Gamaliel. As his student, I was carefully trained in our Jewish laws and customs. I became very zealous to honor God in everything I did, just like all of you today."
> —Acts 22:3

Paul was a Pharisee filled with knowledge of the Torah. The light he had was strong, but it was pharisaic. Metaphorically speaking, many extremely legalistic believers in Christ are immersed in the

Scriptures and cannot see past the light they have so far. So they use Scripture (as they understand it) to defend their views, just as the Pharisees did in Jesus' day.

Too much light can produce scales, and (catch the wordplay) the scales can become unbalanced. When the scales that help you discern right from wrong tip to one side, you become the type of Christian who flashes bright light into other people's eyes and wonders why they resist. Instead of converting them to Christ, you injure them! This is why each of us needs a devout, balanced person like Ananias to hold us accountable and make sure we are not reading the Scriptures in unbalanced, dogmatic ways.

YOU NEED AN ANANIAS

God chose Ananias to help Paul regain his sight. Ananias would also baptize and lay hands on Paul and help clarify the call on Paul's life. Ananias helped Paul find balance.

> Ananias went and found Saul. He laid his hands on him and said, "Brother Saul, the Lord Jesus, who appeared to you on the road, has sent me so that you might regain your sight and be filled with the Holy Spirit." Instantly something like scales fell from Saul's eyes, and he regained his sight. Then he got up and was baptized.
>
> —ACTS 9:17–18

Many people trapped in tradition and legalism have no Ananias to guide them forward. So a church system guides them instead. Years ago I prided myself in allowing the system to guide me. Trust me, you lose all sense of humanity in that kind of arrangement. You become a zealot and acolyte willing to do anything to ensure the rules are obeyed.

I thank God that He brought an Ananias to my wife, Ibelize, and me: Bishop Hugh Daniel Smith of Embassy Covenant Church International currently serves as my overseer and spiritual father.

Like Ananias, he is devout, humble, and honest. He is willing to remind me when I need it; and as Ananias did for Paul, he helps me maintain a godly balance between zeal and love, light and dark.

In all humility, I pray this book allows me to be a kind of Ananias to you. Don't allow the devil to get in your head, convincing you to drop the book. The devil wants all believers to live with scales on their eyes. So please be determined to read this book to the end. Let it open your eyes, and let God set you free from anything that conflicts with the gospel of love and grace. I speak grace, grace to you now!

ERROR AND GNATS

Don't allow the light of legalism to keep you in error. A synonym for *error* is *mistake*. When I read the Word years ago, I made all kinds of mistakes. The reason is simple: I was ignorant. I learned that one mistake can cascade into a series of actions, and the fallout can take years to fix. A life of error can quench God's power on your behalf.

Speaking to the Sadducees about their beliefs concerning life after death, Jesus said, "You do err, not knowing the scriptures, nor the power of God" (Matt. 22:29, KJV). Jesus said straight out that the Sadducees' misreading of Scripture caused them to believe something totally erroneous. When pastors slam women for wearing pants or say someone is going to hell because they attended a soccer game or cut their hair or pierced an ear—they are *in error*.

Straining at gnats

For many years, I asked the Lord how believers can arrive at such erroneous conclusions, when even a momentary removal of their blinders would show they are misguided and misusing context. God's answer was, "They strain out a gnat and swallow a camel." This idea comes from an exchange in which Jesus addressed Pharisees, scribes, and hypocrites, saying, "Blind guides! You strain your water so you won't accidentally swallow a gnat, but you swallow a camel!" (Matt. 23:24). In other words, you work hard to extract the smallest morsel of meaning only to arrive at something God never said.

Straining at gnats leads to extremism. The Bible's warning against the lust of the eyes can cause a pastor to strain out a gnat and create a camel of a rule about throwing out all televisions and cell phones that might cause one's eyes to sin. Now you have a church full of people throwing out their devices, and you convince yourself it was God's idea.

It's not only legalistic Christians who strain out gnats. Many contemporary Jews strain at the command of not working on the Sabbath: In Israel, I was privileged to celebrate the Sabbath in a Jewish man's house. When I asked him why all the lights were turned on, he said they did that ahead of the Sabbath because they're not allowed to turn on the light switch on the day of rest.

Swallowing camels

When Jesus mentioned swallowing camels, He illustrated the futility of straining out gnats. When you are so focused on one tiny detail, you miss the bigger, more important issue. Metaphorically, you end up swallowing a camel, an unclean animal that God's people were forbidden to eat under the law.

Where people and churches are overly taken with tradition, I wonder which bigger issues are being ignored. Let me give you an example, but with this disclaimer: I am not for Christians getting tattoos. As a deliverance minister I have a sense of where tattoos can lead. However, you'll never convince me someone with a Scripture tattoo or a tattoo honoring a deceased loved one is condemned to hell. That idea is not God's; it's legalism—a fine point that distracts people from what is truly important.

I don't want to swallow camels, but I have another, more basic reason not to be legalistic: I am very aware that I've got my own issues before God. (Currently, I'm dealing with surrendering to the

Lord.) I have no business policing my brethren, as God is dealing with us all.

THE MOVEMENT OF THE CIRCUMCISION

Let's look at another group that strained out gnats: the movement of the circumcision. But be warned—I'm about to get a bit stern. There are similarities between the movement of the circumcision (in Paul's day) and today's legalists, and Paul was very stern about the former group.

The traits these groups share are not hard to discover, but let's consider them now.

1. The circumcision required believers to be circumcised *in addition to* believing in Christ. Modern-day legalism requires believers to follow holiness standards *in addition to* believing in Christ.

2. The circumcision continued to uphold the traditions and customs created by men. Modern-day legalism continues to uphold the traditions and customs created by people.

3. The circumcision continued to practice Jewish separation from Gentile believers. Modern-day legalists continue to practice personal separation from Christians whose beliefs they dislike.

4. The circumcision was a movement not sanctioned by the early church. Modern-day legalism is not sanctioned by the larger body of Christ.

5. The circumcision stirred up trouble within the church. Modern-day legalists make trouble within churches.

6. The circumcision followed and persecuted Paul, hoping to undo and discredit his work. Modern-day legalists will follow, discredit, and try to undo churches that don't believe exactly what they do.

This list could go on, but these parallels make my point: The circumcision movement is alive and well today. The same spirit that drove the ancient movement is still at work. Paul contended with that spirit and addressed the circumcision in almost every epistle. He warned Timothy, "Cling to your faith in Christ, and keep your conscience clear. For some people have deliberately violated their consciences; as a result, their faith has been shipwrecked" (1 Tim. 1:19).

The same warning applies to the current legalistic movement: Because many misunderstand and add their own ideas to the Scriptures, they shipwreck faith for themselves and others. Paul told the Corinthian church, "I have applied all these things to myself and Apollos for your benefit, brothers, that you may learn by us not to go beyond what is written" (1 Cor. 4:6, ESV). And notice what happens when you "go beyond what is written": Paul said that "you may be puffed up in favor of one against another" (1 Cor. 4:6, ESV).

Mentioning Paul, Peter also spoke strongly against the kind of ignorance that twists the truth and shipwrecks our faith:

> Count the patience of our Lord as salvation, just as our beloved brother Paul also wrote to you according to the wisdom given him, as he does in all his letters when he speaks in them of these matters. There are some things in them that are hard to understand, which the ignorant and unstable twist to their own destruction, as they do the other Scriptures.
> —2 PETER 3:15–16, ESV

Modern-day legalism adds to what is already written! Paul condemned the practice, and so should we. But let's remember to love the people caught in legalism's grip, even as we hate the doctrine and system that have entangled them.

Assumption and Tradition

So how does one begin to believe it's appropriate to add to what is already written? My answer can be summed up in one word: *assumption*. Assuming things can cause a person to risk being wrong without even realizing it. Notice how Jesus spoke to religious leaders who thought they knew more than He did. Jesus told them, "You search the Scriptures because you think they give you eternal life. But the Scriptures point to me!" (John 5:39).

When Jesus said, "You *think*," He pointed out the assumptions in the Jewish leaders' scholastic approach to the Scriptures. They thought eternal life was found in black letters on white pages. But it is found only in the person who has the authority to give eternal life to anyone He chooses. That person is Jesus!

Futile assumptions are at least as common now as they were in Jesus' day. Many people in our world trust more in their traditions than in divine grace. They have not learned to rest in Christ or His covenant of grace. They strive by way of religion, with many churches assuming that a relationship with God is developed by observing their traditions. Yet God is calling them to an intimate relationship with Him—not through their doing but through the person of His Son, Jesus, by the power of the Holy Spirit.

This is where many churches hit a wall. In order to maintain their traditions, they quench the person of the Holy Spirit and miss the vibrancy of relationship with God the Father. This explains why many (but not all) churches have huge buildings and little anointing. They have millions of dollars in the bank, but their hearts are lukewarm. They have lots of people, but there is sin in the camp. They have many programs and outreaches, but many of their people need deliverance. They've lost the urgency for evangelism but are zealous to enforce the rules and regulations. They shout at messages of condemnation and get excited when judgment hits a believer.

Many of these churches truly mean well, but they are missing the point.

NICODEMUS: THE MYSTERY OF BEING BORN AGAIN

Christianity is about pursuing an intimate relationship with God rather than religion. When you ignore the Holy Spirit, you cannot discern heavenly things, even if you mean well. Consider Nicodemus. He could not understand the spiritual concepts Jesus shared with him—even while Jesus looked him right in the eye! When Jesus said, "Unless one is born again he cannot see the kingdom of God" (John 3:3, ESV), Nicodemus tried to figure out how an old man like himself could pass through his mother's birth canal a second time. Nicodemus's literalism blinded him to what Jesus was sharing.

Nicodemus truly thought the born-again person would be able and required to climb back in the womb. His literalism, his "disposition to take words and statements in their literal sense,"[3] was in full bloom. Therefore, he didn't even attempt to consider Jesus' words metaphorically.

I'm not faulting Nicodemus. In fact, I can relate to him. I remember being too mentally locked up to understand the deep things of God. I tried to sound like I was deep, and I struggled to prepare sermons. Instead of allowing the Spirit to guide me into revelation, I tried to make scriptures fit my sermon titles. Far be it from me to judge Nicodemus! But his example is important, and he wasn't the only person who wrestled with the things Jesus said.

It's not surprising that today's legalists fall into the same trap that got Nicodemus. Without thinking through the context of Old Testament scriptures, they isolate texts and make them mean things that have little or nothing to do with reality or our day and age. For instance, I was in churches where pastors would use Leviticus 14:8— "the persons being purified must then wash their clothes, shave off all their hair, and bathe themselves in water. Then they will be ceremonially clean and may return to the camp"—to tell men they must shave their faces in order to preach, minister, or even be considered Spirit-filled. They used that verse to enforce their own doctrine that men should be clean-shaven. Like Nicodemus, these ministries try to fit God's thoughts into boxes of their own making.

THE PEOPLE: SCARED STIFF BY "CANNIBALISM"

Consider the following words of Jesus, which the people found to be very controversial. We will soon see how they responded.

> "I am the living bread that came down from heaven. If anyone eats of this bread, he will live forever. And the bread that I will give for the life of the world is my flesh." The Jews then disputed among themselves, saying, "How can this man give us his flesh to eat?"
>
> —JOHN 6:51–52, ESV

Jesus continued speaking but only seemed to add fuel to the fire. He said, "My flesh is true food, and my blood is true drink" (John 6:55, ESV). The crowd did what Nicodemus had done: They took Jesus literally. When He said to eat His flesh, they envisioned cannibalism, which was considered an abomination.

I will mercifully assume they became offended because they did not think through what Jesus said. I've been there. I used the term *greasy grace* more than once in my legalistic history. I simply could not assimilate the teaching of grace into my locked-down theology.

The crowd in John 6 could not assimilate Jesus' message either, so they walked away from Him—and Jesus was not surprised. He "knew from the beginning who those were who did not believe, and who it was who would betray him" (John 6:64, ESV). He also knew more people would desert Him before His work was finished. He told the crowd,

> "This is why I told you that no one can come to me unless it is granted him by the Father."
>
> After this many of his disciples turned back and no longer walked with him. So Jesus said to the twelve, "Do you want to go away as well?" Simon Peter answered him, "Lord, to whom shall we go? You have the words of eternal life, and we have believed, and have come to know, that you are the Holy One of God."
>
> —John 6:65–69, ESV

Are you struggling the way Nicodemus or the crowd in John 6 did? If so, I have great news: The Holy Spirit is here to remove the scales from your eyes. Like Paul, you can transition into the grace of God. But you need to trust God in the process. Instead of walking away, yield to the Holy Spirit. Be like Peter in Acts chapter 10—he didn't immediately understand what his vision on the rooftop meant, but he was willing to wait until Jesus clarified it for him.

Even if legalism is all you know, let Jesus show you something beyond what you have been taught. Instead of fearing that grace will lead you to take license, you can rest assured that true biblical grace will help you live holy. "For the grace of God that bringeth salvation hath appeared to all men, teaching us that, denying ungodliness and worldly lusts, we should live soberly, righteously, and godly, in this present world" (Titus 2:11–12, KJV).

KING-JAMES-ONLY PEOPLE

Sometimes the religious mindset tries to control which Bible version you use. I admit I don't recommend all the recent Bible versions for your primary Bible reading, but as secondary sources they can provide a wider perspective.

There are far too many churches insisting that everyone use the King James Version of the Bible. I am aware many consider the authorized 1611 King James Bible to be the closest Bible version to the *Textus Receptus*, "a series of Byzantine based Greek texts of the New Testament printed between 1500 and 1900."[4]

I still use the KJV when I am studying the Bible, and I've used it often in this book. But I also read other versions. When I hear zealous teachers insisting on the King James Version and calling all other versions invalid, I don't hear Holy Spirit wisdom speaking; I hear dogmatism. In some theological camps the controversy is so extreme that it involves whether the third person of the Trinity should be called the *Holy Spirit* or the *Holy Ghost*. Some pastors won't allow you in their churches unless you use the name *Holy Ghost*. This kind of nitpicking goes too far!

Extremism also distresses new believers, causing unnecessary guilt and false anxiety. If you are new to the faith, what matters is that you read the Bible and are learning about Christ. If the Holy Spirit is living inside you, He will guide you into all truth, regardless of the Bible version you use. Be at peace, my brother or sister. Don't let Bible-version puritans disrupt your Bible reading. If the Holy Ghost wants you to change versions, He'll tell you so. The Spirit of truth "will guide you into all the truth, for he will not speak on his own authority, but whatever he hears he will speak, and he will declare to you the things that are to come" (John 16:13, ESV).

LEGALISM PRODUCES FALSE ANXIETY

Anxiety is real. Many people deal with it and take medication for it. But the false anxiety of legalism is something thrust on the saint in order to force a preoccupation with rules. I felt that anxiety when I realized it is impossible for humans to obey all the rules all the time.

You might be familiar with this condition, but its source is a lie. The rules you can't possibly manage are not from Scripture. Nor have they been sanctioned by Jesus, who is the head of the church. Instead, a religious demon is trying to dominate your thoughts. So I urge you to stand on your feet and declare the following words in a strong, firm voice:

I speak to every religious demon that's attacking my mind with false anxiety. I command you, in the name of Jesus, to leave me now and never come back! My life is complete in Christ, and my mind and soul are at peace in Jesus. Demons of legalism, I order you to go now, in the name of Jesus. Holy Spirit, I welcome You to fill my mind, soul, and body with Your presence and God's truth! In Jesus' name, amen.

BREAKING FREE AND MOVING FORWARD

What is the solution when man-made traditions subvert the true understanding of Scripture? I believe the answer is the following verse:

> What sorrow awaits you teachers of religious law and you Pharisees. Hypocrites! For you are careful to tithe even the tiniest [like a gnat] income from your herb gardens, but you ignore the more important aspects of the law—justice, mercy, and faith. You should tithe, yes, but do not neglect the more important things.
> —MATTHEW 23:23

Jesus laid out three aspects of the law that religion tends to lump together. These aspects—justice, mercy, and faith—trump some of the minor, insignificant rules we hold dear. When these three dominate your worldview, you will find yourself getting free of legalism. So let's take a look.

1. Justice

I am so glad justice is first, because without justice a legal system is neither fair nor reasonable. Religious systems are often unfair. Think of how women are labeled as Jezebels or Delilahs. They are treated harshly, while men seem to get away with so much. (Notice I said *seem*.) But anyone can be trapped by injustice. Do you remember when Pilate wanted to let Jesus go because He was innocent? Then the chief priest reminded Pilate that Jesus claimed to be the King. The chief priest trapped Pilate in a legal technicality that could cost him his position and life. The religious system perverted justice and forced Pilate to have Jesus crucified.

You may be aware of injustices playing out in today's church. Maybe a young lady got pregnant out of wedlock and was disciplined harshly, but when the pastor's daughter committed the same sin, her sentence was much lighter. What about the head keyboardist who was found sleeping around with women, but the leadership turned a blind eye because the church relied so heavily on its musicians? Meanwhile, another man in the church was shamed and possibly excommunicated for his sin.

As the Holy Spirit shifts your understanding of the law and opens your eyes to the true meaning of God's Word, you become fair in your dealings with others and with yourself. You reflect the character of our just God, and you help your church be a place of justice. Instead of being patient and loving with outsiders and harsh within the church, you become fair to all people.

2. Mercy

Mercy is so necessary in the transition out of legalism—and for good reasons! You're going to make lots of mistakes as you implement what God has outlined in Scripture, and mercy gives you room to realize and correct your mistakes. The legalistic system allows no such room. "Anyone who has set aside the law of Moses dies without mercy on the evidence of two or three witnesses" (Heb. 10:28, ESV). The lack of mercy is why certain people in the Old Testament were stoned over minor infractions. Lawbreakers were always guilty of punishment.

Because the law was so rigid, many sacrifices were made and many offerings given under the Old Testament. Their purpose was to cover the sins of the ignorant. Numbers 15:24 even describes a sacrifice and offering on behalf of those who committed unintentional sins. I love this verse because it shows that mercy rather than judgment is our heavenly Father's way. James 2:13 says that "mercy triumphs over judgment" (ESV), and Jesus said, "I desire mercy, not sacrifice" (Hos. 6:6, NIV).

In your journey to overcome toxic religion, God will reveal His mercy, and you will become merciful toward yourself and others who don't measure up! Remember, only Jesus is perfect. The rest of us need mercy, and He extended it. Mercy will overcome the religious spirit!

3. Faith

The third major aspect of the law is faith. We humans are heavily influenced by our feelings, but faith is not a feeling. It takes faith to express mercy and justice! As creatures entangled in how we feel, we don't always feel like being gracious, merciful, fair, or just. Faith means believing what God said and being determined to act on it regardless of how we feel.

This aspect of the law was especially hard for me. I knew what God said about grace, but I felt enslaved to a fire-and-brimstone culture. In the harshest church settings I would forget what I was learning about grace, and I would binge on being religious. When I caught myself, I would try to snap out of my binge. I would ask for forgiveness and would walk by faith! It was hard to do, but it became easier over time. I realized my faith was pleasing to God and my legalism was not. I encourage you to ask the Holy Spirit to help you walk in justice, mercy, and faith!

Renew your mind

Breaking free from the clutches of tradition takes reprogramming. My worldview and my wife's had much in common that was shaped by wrong theology. The only way to change that was to unlearn everything. We needed deconstruction and detoxification. Both came from leaning on Jesus, opening our eyes to the Scripture's true meaning, and standing on God's Word. We did not need behavior modification; we needed heart and mind transformation.

Romans 12:2 tells us, "Do not be conformed to this world, but be transformed by the renewal of your mind, that by testing you may discern what is the will of God, what is good and acceptable and perfect" (ESV). Once your thinking changes and you view Scripture in its proper context, you get free from the religious echo chamber, and God shows you His will. Because of wrong theology, God's will seems mysterious to many people. But when you align yourself with true biblical theology, you can preach the gospel to the lost and help grow the churches.

The renewed mind is essential, but it takes time. Hasty changes are usually a sign of Band-Aid-type solutions. The religious mindset is stubborn and stiff-necked. It does not change easily, and it requires much time spent in Scripture to soften it! Then you will understand God's will and not be driven by rules and regulations.

Renew your spirit

Scripture talks about not only renewing your mind but also renewing the spirit of your mind. The word translated "spirit" here refers to a "disposition" or attitude.[5] When the mind changes, attitudes also need to change. Stressing the contrast between the new creation and the old self, Paul urged believers not to have callous hearts:

> That is not the way you learned Christ!—assuming that you have heard about him and were taught in him, as the truth is in Jesus, to put off your old self, which belongs to your former manner of life and is corrupt through deceitful desires, and to be renewed in the spirit of your minds, and to put on the new self, created after the likeness of God in true righteousness and holiness.
>
> —EPHESIANS 4:20–24, ESV

As you genuinely seek freedom from legalism, you will learn to drop your legalistic thoughts and expunge your legalistic attitudes—the religious demeanor and self-righteousness that seep out of the pores and form a cloud around the legalistic Christian.

God wants to deliver you from that and leave no trace of it. Sometimes when people get around my wife and me and hear us expressing jubilance and the joy of the Lord, they can't tell that we came from such a strict religious background. When God took us out of that environment, our attitudes changed, and you can't tell what we used to be!

If that's not your story yet, I believe it will be. God has a powerful assignment for you to accomplish, but it's not about enforcing rules. It's about being a fisher of men! Whether you're the preacher in the pulpit or the person in the pew, God is extending grace toward you so you can be free of legalism. He's already upgrading your understanding of the Scriptures and detoxing your perspectives. He will continue to open your eyes to the wonderful hidden truths you desire, and legalism will be a thing of the past.

Chapter 5

MISPLACED ZEAL AND RULE-FREE RIGHTEOUSNESS

The longing of my heart and my prayer to God is for the people of Israel to be saved. I know what enthusiasm they have for God, but it is misdirected zeal.
—Romans 10:1–2

As we delve into the subject of zeal, bear this in mind: Hyper-anything is toxic and dangerous in the kingdom. In postmodern Christianity this statement might go against the grain in some quarters. However, Scripture makes it clear that self-control and gentleness are prized kingdom qualities. Paul explained why: "A servant of the Lord must not quarrel but must be kind to everyone, be able to teach, and be patient with difficult people. Gently instruct those who oppose the truth. Perhaps God will change those people's hearts, and they will learn the truth" (2 Tim. 2:24–25).

The previous passage refutes the current spiritual climate. About one hundred years after the Azusa Street Revival, the Christian life seems centered around passion, excitement, and jubilance. These things are not wrong, but there is a sense of hyperexpectation about them. Unless our worship celebrations are filled with intense passion and emotion, we conclude God "wasn't in the house." If a service seems to be dry or somehow boring, we look for ways to spice it up with zeal.

If I seem to be painting with a broad brush, please forgive me. But a significant segment of the church worships at the feet of zeal, and I will be blunt about it. I have never seen so many of God's people given over to the concept. And in recent years, I have seen believers engage in some of the weirdest, most bizarre antics, all in the name of passion and emotion.

Unbridled zeal doesn't glorify God; it promotes a version of Christianity I call *Weirdo Christianity*. I believe that, at times, God will have you say or do something that is out of the norm. But when God is behind it, whatever is said or done will draw attention to Jesus—not to you or what you are doing. Much of what God is credited with doing is nothing more than man-made, emotionally generated zeal that has little or nothing to do with Him. Therefore, a corrective word is in order.

LED BY THE SPIRIT, NOT DRIVEN

Let's establish the important idea that God is not looking for everything He does or says to be extreme. Yes, God does some radical things. Yet after a dramatic windstorm, earthquake, and fire, God spoke to Elijah in "a still small voice" (1 Kings 19:12, KJV). The previous verse states that "the LORD was not in the wind...the LORD was not in the earthquake" (1 Kings 19:11), and verse 12 says that He "was not in the fire" either (KJV).

This is important because New Testament believers are not to be driven; we are meant to be led. The driven person is so focused on what they're doing that it blinds them to everything and everyone around them. Have you ever witnessed someone whose zeal is so great they have no concept of others? I have. Their fanaticism can become so exaggerated that anyone who tries to counsel them becomes a target of attack.

Unregulated zeal hurts the church and people. An example is

a church group I mentioned earlier: the Rabakukus. This name was given to them by the larger community; it's a sarcastic term inspired by their extreme behavior. Their videos, which are all over YouTube, show church leaders preaching, shouting, and screaming while running alongside people's cars in the middle of traffic. One of the main leaders within this movement was known as *soporte mi locura* (translation: "Can you handle my craziness?"). He has since left the movement and publicly apologized for his fanaticism.

If you are member of Los Rabakukus or Westboro Baptist Church, or any other radical congregation, please understand that Spirit-filled Christians are not driven; they are led by the Spirit who gives self-control as fruit. Self-control is not our enemy; it is essential to being used in the gifts of the Spirit.

The Meaning and Source of Zeal

Romans 12:11 says, "Do not be slothful in zeal, be fervent in spirit, serve the Lord" (ESV). In English the word *zeal* speaks of ardor and fervency. In the biblical sense this implies a sound but intense devotion. However, this zeal can grow cold over time, and fervency can turn to a kind of stoicism that doesn't attract people to Christ or keep people in the faith.

When zeal moves beyond soundness to an all-out, overboard, and misdirected fanaticism, something is wrong. Consider this example: Some legalistic churches are in dreadful fear of becoming slothful. Therefore, they fiercely attack any perceived lack of zeal, and they frantically try to fan zeal's flame. I have often seen this in churches that stress being on fire for God or radical for God. Yes, we are to be on fire and radical for God, but when we replace Spirit-led zeal with emotion-driven passion, we end up producing a counterfeit form of fervor. And that eventually causes zeal to flame out completely, instead of smoldering for a lifetime.

One biblical personality displayed a level of unregulated zeal unmatched by any other. It was the apostle Paul, before his conversion. He said of himself, "I was far ahead of my fellow Jews in my zeal for the traditions of my ancestors" (Gal. 1:14). Basically, Paul said nobody was more zealous than he was. But he also provided a glimpse into how destructive zeal can be when it is unaccompanied by revelation that is outlined in Scripture and inspired by the Holy Spirit. Paul's untethered zeal was a weapon Satan used to persecute the church.

Zeal can make you violent toward anyone who doesn't measure up to the standard you have in mind. Paul said, "You know what I was like when I followed the Jewish religion—how I violently persecuted God's church. I did my best to destroy it" (Gal. 1:13). Paul's zeal was dangerous and caused him to tolerate and enact violence against Jesus' followers.

But where did Paul's zeal originate? The answer is *in tradition*. For Paul that included the Law of Moses, with all the rules and regulations handed down by Paul's Jewish ancestors. Thankfully, Paul's honesty about his zeal now shows us how to avoid or overcome our own misguided zeal, which often expresses a desire to preserve what we think is dying or being assaulted by change. In the legalistic system the threat of change can trigger violent campaigns against those who favor reforms. Sometimes it simply results in people being voted out of the church.

You may have been in the league with leaders who voted out your pastor or any elders because they didn't follow the bylaws. If so, you need to repent for your divisive behavior. I have seen yearly election meetings turn sour because one or two overzealous brethren raised an issue or objection concerning the bylaws.

Sometimes people in high places have ignored the votes cast for department heads. I remember being voted into a certain position by a landslide but being set aside because a certain bishop took issue with my application of the leadership bylaws. As it turned out, he objected to my belief that women in church should be allowed to wear slacks, and men should be allowed to grow beards!

You could say that the integral voting system within my

denomination was violently assaulted by an overzealous bishop who believed he was doing the right thing. Saul of Tarsus believed persecuting Christians was also the right thing to do—in his eyes and God's! Misguided in his legalism, Saul did whatever seemed necessary to preserve the tradition of his Jewish ancestors. From that mindset even murder was acceptable. So Saul watched as Stephen was brutally murdered. The Jewish leaders "put their hands over their ears and began shouting. They rushed at [Stephen] and dragged him out of the city and began to stone him. His accusers took off their coats and laid them at the feet of a young man named Saul" (Acts 7:57–58).

Paul presented the personal side of his error, showing just how far zeal can take you:

> I used to believe that I ought to do everything I could to oppose the very name of Jesus the Nazarene. Indeed, I did just that in Jerusalem. Authorized by the leading priests, I caused many believers there to be sent to prison. And I cast my vote against them when they were condemned to death.
>
> —Acts 26:9–10

Paul was sincere in his zeal, but he was also sincerely wrong. If you have been abused by overzealous leaders or endured a theological public lynching, know this: God will exchange your ashes for beauty and heal every church hurt you have carried. So go ahead—raise your hands, and receive the power to forgive as the healing balm of Gilead restores every part of your soul. My prayer is that by the time you finish reading this book, you will have regained the healthy fire for God that persecution tried to strip away. Let God's promise to Israel speak to you today:

> To all who mourn in Israel, he will give a crown of beauty for ashes, a joyous blessing instead of mourning, festive praise instead of despair. In their righteousness, they will be like great oaks that the Lord has planted for his own glory. They

will rebuild the ancient ruins, repairing cities destroyed long ago. They will revive them, though they have been deserted for many generations.

—Isaiah 61:3–4

Digging Deeper into Zeal

The subject of zeal could fill a whole series of books. We won't go that deep, but let's take a look at three ways in which misguided zeal manifests, according to Paul's description of himself in his first letter to Timothy:

> I thank him who has given me strength, Christ Jesus our Lord, because he judged me faithful, appointing me to his service, though formerly I was a *blasphemer, persecutor,* and *insolent opponent*. But I received mercy because I had acted ignorantly in unbelief.
> —1 Timothy 1:12–13, esv, emphasis added

The blasphemer

To blaspheme might not mean exactly what we typically think it does. Blaspheming is not only swearing or using God's name in vain. I find it interesting that a blasphemer is also "a person who speaks about God or the holy things of a particular religion in an offensive way."[1]

Most (but not all) zealous believers who are intensely legalistic tend to be offensive in their preaching, teaching, and mannerisms toward other believers. In their zeal they become harsh and even vindictive while preaching holiness, of all things. And yes—I was guilty as charged! I was offensive and known for my brash style of preaching. That is how I was trained in the legalistic churches I came from, and I'm still detoxing from that approach.

Before his conversion Paul was offensive in his dealings with the early church. We know the story in part, but imagine how Paul must have offended the early followers of Christ. Amazingly, I never made the connection between misguided zeal and the offensive ways in which Paul and others throughout Christian history have expressed their faith. What's even crazier is that offensive, overzealous Christians assume they are suffering for Christ. In reality they are suffering for their offenses toward other people!

The persecutor

For the past thirty years my understanding of *persecutor* lacked an important piece that explains how wrong behaviors can slip into our lives when we are sure that we're serving God. If you see yourself as a watchman, for example, this missing piece might be in your repertoire. If so, you might be a persecutor: "a person who treats another person or group of people in a cruel and unfair way"![2]

Are you shocked to hear that cruelty is at the persecutor's center? I was! Even if cruelty does not seem blatant, a lack of tolerance can often be cruel. I am not talking about refusing to tolerate false doctrine. That is something we must do. When lies are presented as truth, we need to refute them. But when persecution revolves around opinions and personal convictions, we overstep our bounds. Many legalistic believers push their personal ideas about holiness, tongues, and deliverance, for example. When they oppose their brethren in the faith concerning these matters of interpretation, they unwittingly becoming persecutors, and that is cruel.

The insolent opponent

The word *insolent* escaped me for many years, but when I searched it out, conviction hit me hard. An insolent person is "extremely rude and showing a lack of respect."[3] If that doesn't depict our day and age, I don't know what does. Rudeness is now the norm, or, in my way of coining a phrase, it ain't safe in these Christian streets.

I believe unregulated zeal is fueling the church's increasing rudeness and lack of respect. If a seasoned minister who's been serving many years misspeaks online, the sharks sense blood in the water, and here they come, ready to slice and dice another believer. Social media platforms such as Facebook, X, and YouTube have become like the Roman Colosseum, with believers being thrown in to fight lions.

This kind of brutality is not new. In the Epistle to the Philippians, Paul described his pre-conversion attitudes toward himself and toward those with whom he disagreed:

> I could have confidence in my own effort if anyone could. Indeed, if others have reason for confidence in their own efforts, I have even more! I was circumcised when I was eight days old. I am a pure-blooded citizen of Israel and a member of the tribe of Benjamin—a real Hebrew if there ever was one! I was a member of the Pharisees, who demand the strictest obedience to the Jewish law. I was so zealous that I harshly persecuted the church. And as for righteousness, I obeyed the law without fault. I once thought these things were valuable, but now I consider them worthless because of what Christ has done.
> —PHILIPPIANS 3:4–7

Notice what Paul valued before his encounter with Christ:

» His breeding, training, and commitment to the law made him a confident man (proud of his résumé).

» He was a proud Pharisee who demanded strict compliance from others, was zealous, and persecuted the church.

» He considered himself faultless in obeying the law.

Like those on social media platforms who call one another "reprobates" and "children of the devil" or predict that "the devil will take them away," Paul deeply disrespected those he saw as opponents. This type of callousness has flourished in recent years, and, until recently, I was trying to figure out what the reason might be.

I know it's a grim picture to present, but we seem to be looking for reasons to argue. And I did say that I would be blunt regarding zeal.

Back to my question about the reason for the uptick in callousness: I believe I found the answer when I looked up the word *insolent*. Remember, it means "extremely rude and showing a lack of respect."[4] When I first read that definition, I trembled because it describes the sin that has permeated the current generation, especially online. However, I am also aware of the legalism and unregulated zeal that often fuel our insolence.

If you see in yourself any of the characteristics Paul found in himself (whether in 1 Timothy 1:12–13 or Philippians 3:4–7), I urge you to get on your knees, repent, and ask God to forgive you—not someday but today.

MISGUIDED ZEAL AND COMPLEXES

Two more causes of misguided zeal deserve honorable mentions here because they seem to be on the rise among church folks who take on the zeal mantle: They are the persecution complex and the rejection complex. I cannot be exhaustive here, but we can tackle them succinctly and gain insight.

Persecution complex

As I write this, most of the Western church isn't under the kind of persecution we read about in the Book of Acts. Yet many believers feel persecuted for their beliefs, particularly (1) those who lean toward legalism, and (2) those who are very opinionated about their own convictions.

Because the current culture encourages us to ask questions, questions are continually being asked, in every field of endeavor. This causes some people to assume they are under persecution from people who disagree with them. But let me offer you this advice: Just because someone disagrees with you or even publicly criticizes you doesn't mean you're persecuted. You might be suffering from a persecution complex—the belief that the whole world is against you because of your convictions and views.

Legalistic believers tend to become defensive and struggle in this area. When I first presented deliverance on social media (circa 2010), I received fierce criticism (and I still do). I remember taking it very personally and firing back publicly. I felt I was being martyred for the ministry of deliverance. So naturally I saw questions and skepticism as being unjust. This stirred a misguided zeal in my heart, and I responded by proselytizing about deliverance. Why? Because my conviction told me no one would stop me.

Oh, how wrong I was! God allowed me to go through something to humble me and slow me down. After many hours of prayer and seeking Him, I got delivered from my persecution complex, and my misguided zeal waned.

Rejection complex

A history of consistent rejection can set up any human being to embrace a rejection complex. Recurring rejection fills a person's heart to the point where everything they say and do is fueled by feelings of rejection. People in this situation are driven to lash out and silence their critics, whether by slandering them or pointing out their flaws. Some people with a rejection complex believe it's their duty to expose other people's flaws.

In all fairness a rejection complex feeds unregulated zeal, which then seeks an outlet by leveling (or trying to level) the playing field and fixing (or trying to fix) partiality and hypocrisy within the church. Unfortunately, such efforts are not inspired by the Holy Spirit. In fact, there is something pharisaic about them, which is why I think Paul mentioned his accolades as a Pharisee in the passage from Philippians 3. Understanding the role his training and grooming in the Law of Moses played in his actions against the church helps us avoid similar pitfalls.

MISGUIDED ZEAL IN ACTION

During one of our Sunday services when I was pastoring Amazing Church Global in New York City, the presence of God was tangible, people were getting saved, and the worship was amazing. As was my custom, I went to the back of the church to provide oversight and ensure things didn't get out of hand. Standing next to me was a gentleman from our church who told another brother, "I'm crazy—I'm crazy for Jesus. Watch me be crazy for Jesus!"

Then, suddenly and erratically, the gentleman began jumping around. It grieved me because there seemed to be no devotion to God. All I could see was a man's effort to break out of fear and put himself in a radical state of mind. It was even more heartbreaking because this gentleman truly loved the Lord (and still does). But he was misguided in that moment, and instead of centering on God, he focused on himself and what he could do for God.

The man's self-centered zeal continued throughout the worship and taught me this lesson: Everything we do needs to be *in Him* and not *for Him*! I never corrected this brother; quite frankly he was still immature in his faith, and correcting him would have crushed him. Looking back, however, I might have considered addressing his misguided zeal, which distracted from worship.

Another example of misguided zeal occurred during the early days of the COVID-19 pandemic, when churches from all over the United States conducted times of fasting and prayer. I remember someone contacting me and asking whether I would be willing to do some strategic prayer over their city to rebuke the spirit of COVID-19. I replied, "God hasn't authorized me to do that."

The person said, "We have authority in Christ, and we can bind and loose."

"Yes, we can," I responded, "but only if God authorizes it."

Then came the sharp answer: "I can't believe your unbelief, brother. You're the deliverance guy!"

"I can't change what you think, but I'm not going to warfare unless God has sent me."

The situation turned into an argument, with the person getting offended and telling me how much my being scared of COVID-19 disappointed them. "You're no longer my hero," they said, and the insults kept coming.

The words got so fierce that I had to correct this person and end the relationship. COVID-19 didn't disappear but became a pandemic, and this person drifted from church and (from what I heard) began hopping from one church to another.

When zeal is misplaced, we assume things that God hasn't said or told us to do, and we open ourselves to error and disappointment.

UNREGULATED ZEAL PRODUCES MADNESS

Another biblical personality whose zeal was unrestrained in my view is Jehu. In 2 Kings 9 we see Elisha sending one of the sons of the prophets to anoint Jehu as king of Israel and to instruct him to bring down Ahab and Jezebel. Jehu was sanctioned by God to end Jezebel's reign, but in my opinion he became bloodthirsty and told Jehonadab, "'Come with me and see my zeal for the LORD.' Then he had him ride along in his chariot" (2 Kings 10:16, NIV).

Various interpretations of Jehu's executions are possible, but I believe he became unrestrained with the authority God gave him—to the point that he began to abuse it and exhibit a kind of madness. We read in the Book of Hosea: "The LORD said, 'Name the child Jezreel, for I am about to punish King Jehu's dynasty to avenge the murders he committed at Jezreel. In fact, I will bring an end to Israel's independence'" (Hos. 1:4). I believe this indicates that Jehu's abuse was so great that he went beyond the assignment of killing Ahab and Jezebel and also killed "all who were left of Ahab's relatives living in Jezreel and all his important officials, his personal friends, and his priests" (2 Kings 10:11).

In fact, "when Jehu came to Samaria, he killed all who were left there of Ahab's family; he destroyed them, according to the word of the LORD spoken to Elijah" (2 Kings 10:17, NIV). These actions might seem warranted because God wanted Ahab and Jezebel dead. But following specific instructions is crucially important. I propose that Jehu's zeal got the best of him, and ultimately brought judgment from God (Hos. 1:4).

Unregulated zeal always causes us to go beyond what God mandates. God does not sanction what New Yorkers call being "extra." He sanctions our obedience.

ZEALOTS AT WORK

Unrestrained zeal has many side effects. Perhaps the most apparent is the judgmental, critical attitude that targets the demise of people who make mistakes or disagree with the zealot. We see this brand of bloodlust in John chapter 8:

> The scribes and the Pharisees brought a woman who had been caught in adultery, and placing her in the midst they said to him, "Teacher, this woman has been caught in the act of adultery. Now in the Law, Moses commanded us to stone such women. So what do you say?"
>
> —JOHN 8:3–5, ESV

We saw earlier how Jesus reminded the woman's accusers of their own sin. He also described this dynamic during His Sermon on the Mount. In very visual terms He warned against being overly critical of others and forgetting how sinful we are.

> Why worry about a speck in your friend's eye when you have a log in your own? How can you think of saying to your friend, "Let me help you get rid of that speck in your eye," when you can't see past the log in your own eye? Hypocrite! First get rid of the log in your own eye; then you will see well enough to deal with the speck in your friend's eye.
>
> —MATTHEW 7:3–5

In the Book of Romans, Paul also pinpointed the Jewish believers' tendency to criticize what they saw as other people's wrongdoing. Paul rebuked the legalistic Jews' hypocrisy in following the law externally but potentially violating it internally.

> Indeed you are called a Jew, and rest on the law, and make your boast in God, and know His will, and approve the things that are excellent, being instructed out of the law, and are confident that you yourself are a guide to the blind, a light to those who are in darkness, an instructor of the foolish, a teacher of babes, having the form of knowledge and truth in the law. You, therefore, who teach another, do you not teach yourself? You who preach that a man should not steal, do you steal? You who say, "Do not commit adultery," do you commit adultery?
>
> —Romans 2:17–22, nkjv

For people who wanted to be known as champions of holiness and God's own police force, Paul's upbraiding surely hit home. As Jesus said, "Let the one who has never sinned throw the first stone!" (John 8:7).

Peter's Misguided Zeal

One thing I won't be guilty of is deifying biblical personalities. Outside Jesus Christ (who is God manifested in the flesh) the people in Scripture were human, prone to mistakes, and given to extremes. The apostle Paul wasn't the only one who struggled with unregulated zeal. Peter also had zealous tendencies.

The church often highlights Peter's strengths, but we need to acknowledge his weaknesses. First, we find Peter promising never to betray Jesus, saying, "Lord, I am ready to go to prison with you, and even to die with you" (Luke 22:33). Only a person given over to zeal is quick to declare what they would or would not do in a situation they have not yet faced. We know that later, during Jesus' passion, Peter in fact denied Jesus—three times. In his zeal he made a promise he would not keep.

The second time Peter's zeal got the best of him was when Jesus was about to wash his feet, and Peter resisted. In my estimation Peter's response came from a place of extreme zeal. Yet in fairness to him, he quickly changed his tune.

> "No," Peter protested, "you will never ever wash my feet!" Jesus replied, "Unless I wash you, you won't belong to me." Simon Peter exclaimed, "Then wash my hands and head as well, Lord, not just my feet!"
> —JOHN 13:8–9

Peter was being extra, a man of extremes. So once he understood Jesus' point, he went overboard and said, "Wash my hands and head as well." Peter's zeal was still not quenched, however. When Judas led a contingent of Roman soldiers and temple guards to Jesus, Peter "drew a sword and slashed off the right ear of Malchus, the high priest's slave. But Jesus said to Peter, 'Put your sword back into its sheath. Shall I not drink from the cup of suffering the Father has given me?'" (John 18:10–11).

Talk about being consumed by zeal! I personally doubt Peter was aiming for Malchus's ear, but that's neither here nor there. What seems stunning is that Peter assumed the slicing off of someone's ear to be a logical response. Jesus immediately let him know God is not pleased by anyone "going hard for God." It was time to put down the sword.

Rule-Free Righteousness

This topic is short and to the point: Those who come out of extremely legalistic environments often become rebels, not only against legalism but also against righteousness. The following examples explain what I mean.

1. Some men forced to wear suits choose never to wear them again, not even for interviews, funerals, or special occasions that require such attire.
2. Some women forced to wear long skirts later choose to wear tight and even provocative clothing.
3. Some women forbidden to wear earrings end up wearing very elaborate earrings.
4. People forced to study, teach, and enforce extreme doctrine often end up perpetuating and embracing false doctrine.
5. People forced into conservative doctrines regarding issues such as homosexuality can end up embracing extremely tolerant worldviews.
6. Many men forced to shave their beards as a sign of holiness end up growing long beards and long hair, and some add earrings.
7. Young people forced to listen to only Christian music often end up using their gifts and talents for the world at large. (Many of today's gifted musicians started in the church.)

These extremes are not caused only by legalism, but throughout my years as a Christian and a minister I have seen that where holiness is pushed the hardest, church members are most apt to push back, often in favor of rule-free righteousness.

Let me explain what I mean by *rule-free righteousness*. It's a response from people who have been hurt by a system of rules: Instead of becoming zealous rule-keepers, they tend to become extremely zealous about ignoring the rules. They are quick to call something legalistic, and the moment they are challenged by a sermon or situation that holds them to an appropriate higher standard, they write it off as legalist manipulation.

Have you ever met people in that crowd? I have. Many (but not all) of them are the children of pastors and church leaders. It is not uncommon for them to leave the church altogether. Many pastors have retired with saddened hearts because their children either refused the mantle, never heard the call to ministry, or wandered from God. Being raised in negative religion can kill any desire your children might have to serve God! And in their zeal against negative religion, they become legalistic about not being legalists.

Legalistic rules and regulations make even appropriate standards unattractive. I saw this with some of the men in our church who never dressed up for special functions, even if it was requested. Others avoided the issue by not showing up at all. Even some newly ordained ministers became careless with their appearance. I talked to them behind closed doors and said, "We're not legalistic in this church, but I would like for our ministers to look presentable and modest."

I chuckle as I write about this because one of our minsters asked, "Why?" We both had a good, hard laugh because he was dead serious. So I explained from the Scriptures the difference between holiness and righteousness.

Having been in ministry since 1995, I've seen another dismal effect of legalism that affects many people and causes some of them to reach out to our ministry for help. The issue is an epidemic of younger megachurch pastors experiencing personal failures in public ways. I have sat with many, a large percentage of whom come from extremely legalistic backgrounds. When they became pastors, they vowed never to lead their churches like the churches in which they were raised.

Unfortunately, this approach produces the desire for a rule-free culture, where the dangers of sin aren't preached and hell is never discussed. These younger leaders and their churches have embraced only the pleasant aspects of the gospel and have ignored the more difficult realities. This type of culture is very present in today's church, and it's apparent all over social media. It is resistant to any scrutiny over questionable practices or methods of evangelism. If you raise a concern, leaders and others from these churches turn defensive and say, "We're not into legalism."

This common, pat answer might cause some people to let the issue go. But as answers go, it does not hold water. Look what the apostle Paul said about this perspective, not once but twice:

> You say, "I am allowed to do anything"—but not everything is good for you. And even though "I am allowed to do anything," I must not become a slave to anything.
> —1 Corinthians 6:12

> You say, "I am allowed to do anything"—but not everything is good for you. You say, "I am allowed to do anything"—but not everything is beneficial. Don't be concerned for your own good but for the good of others.
> —1 Corinthians 10:23–24

These texts are saying that because of grace, Christ affords the believer a measure of freedom, but we are to handle that freedom responsibly. If freedom enslaves you to a so-called rule-free ideology or any unbiblical ideology, Paul clearly stated that your freedom is both self-centered and unprofitable.

We can choose to say, "That's between me and God" or "That's not my fault" or "The Holy Spirit doesn't convict me on such matters." But the passages we just read present a higher standard and hold us accountable for our effect on our brothers and sisters. Far be it from us to become stumbling blocks to them!

Breaking Free and Moving Forward

Have these pages helped you discern a misguided zeal or sense of rule-free righteousness in your own life? Have the examples reminded you of questionable things you have done or said in the past? Or perhaps they have inspired you to reflect on any damage that has resulted from rules you have enforced that went beyond the scope of what God has called you to do.

Take stock

Remember that in his zeal Paul physically killed Christians. You might be online "killing" with words the brethren who differ from you. Have you taken issue to the point of publicly trying to discredit them? Maybe you're a pastor who has stressed bylaws so harshly that people have walked away—not just from your church but from the church, and from the Lord.

Never forget: God is a God of mercy. If you have done any of those things, own them! Admit your extreme zeal and legalism. Confess to yourself and to God that you have hurt people. God will forgive you! You might need to make some apologies and make things right with folks, but the Holy Spirit will guide you.

Receive mercy

Paul did some terrible things, yet his story ended beautifully. Even as he traveled to persecute God's church, the Lord Jesus appeared to him on the Damascus road and opened his eyes to the error of his ways.

> Then [Saul] fell to the ground, and heard a voice saying to him, "Saul, Saul, why are you persecuting Me?" And he said, "Who are You, Lord?" Then the Lord said, "I am Jesus, whom you are persecuting. It is hard for you to kick against the goads."
> —Acts 9:4–5, NKJV

The Lord Jesus extended His mercy toward Saul and gave him a revelation of Himself that radically changed Saul's life. This single event transformed the man, and he became one of the greatest apostles in spreading the gospel. My point is this: If you are legalistic, don't worry, and don't condemn yourself. The Lord already knows about all that. But He is continually softening your heart. I believe by the time you finish this book, the Holy Spirit will give you such a revelation of Jesus that it will transform *your* life.

Look ahead in hope

If you are a bishop overseeing a denomination or a movement of churches, I foresee you calling a solemn assembly of all your churches and addressing the legalism that's killing your movement. I see you addressing the zeal that's causing many dear people to leave and attend other churches. I pray that you will decree changes in your movement's bylaws and dogmas, and I look forward to hearing about a revival like none your denomination has ever known. Don't be surprised if—within two years' time—the number of churches in your denomination doubles.

Maybe you're not in your church's leadership, but God is dealing with you about your unrestrained zeal. God is already touching your mind. Do you sense the Lord taking the scales off your eyes and giving you the mind of Christ? Hallelujah! He is replacing your zeal with glory. Yes, He will do this—*for you!*

> *Lord, I sense Your guiding hand, and I'm hearing Your voice in a new way. Thank You for opening my eyes more and more each day. Please continue to lead me into the freedom You desire for me, and help me be a vessel of honor who loves Your people well. Thank You for Your mercy and for meeting me where I am. I am so grateful for where I've been and where You are leading me. In Jesus' name, amen.*

Chapter 6

MISUSE OF AUTHORITY

Yet it isn't I who will accuse you before the Father. Moses will accuse you! Yes, Moses, in whom you put your hopes.
—JOHN 5:45

MOSES IS A key biblical personality. So we now revisit him in a more in-depth way. After Jesus Christ and John the Baptist, I believe that Moses is the most important and most influential prophet who ever lived. I realize Elijah holds this position for many believers, but Elijah wrote no books and left no known memoir for his disciples. Yet thousands of years later Moses's influence is still dominant in Israel, Judaism, and Christianity.

In chapter 2 we looked into veneration. In this chapter we will explore (1) how the children of Israel venerated Moses, and (2) how this veneration and an extreme honor culture are paralleled in the relationship between some legalistic churches and their leaders. But please understand that nothing I say here is intended to dishonor Moses or his memory. I am simply trying to convey how the worship of leaders can and does exist in the church, most virulently within cultic communities, but more mildly in legalistic church settings.

For example, in the Latino churches I attended, the pastor was the voice of God for the church and was seen as the congregation's father figure. No changes within the church were permitted without the approval of the pastor or his wife. This included the most minute details involving the placement of chairs, the choice of trash cans, the people's attire, and the freedom to visit other churches. The pastor had to be consulted in every matter, including the people's marital and employment decisions, and his authorization or permission was needed. Unless you had the pastor's approval, your decisions were "not blessed."

Those who attend certain legalistic Latino churches can vouch for what I am saying. Yet they often don't see their level of submission as cultish or overly venerating. They believe they are rightly honoring their pastor, which is part of the Latino culture.

As you know by now, I take issue with such forms of veneration, and calling it out is not a form of rebelling. I am pointing out, righteously in my opinion, that such rules are not true to the gospel of Jesus Christ. The veneration of clergy, other church leaders, movement founders, and other prominent figures in the body of Christ should be questioned.

This type of veneration doesn't develop overnight but starts out as genuine loyalty based on the leader's vision. In time, however, it moves toward the extreme honor model and borders on human idolatry. This dynamic hinders spiritual growth and discourages people from leaving legalistic systems. Why? Because they don't want to disappoint or hurt their leaders! They remain committed to the "man or woman of God," even when they disagree doctrinally.

Venerating Moses: Insights

Israel's veneration of Moses took time to develop as supernatural events occurred. God openly endorsed His servant. Moses was considered to be the meekest man in all the earth. (See Numbers 12:3, KJV.) But the people around him were not as close to God as he was. They held Moses in such high regard that he had to remind them he was just a man. Even Joshua had to be corrected when he became offended over two elders who prophesied within the camp:

> Eldad and Medad....were listed among the elders, but they had not gone out to the Tabernacle. Yet the Spirit rested upon them as well, so they prophesied there in the camp. A young man ran and reported to Moses, "Eldad and Medad are prophesying in the camp!" Joshua son of Nun, who had been Moses' assistant since his youth, protested, "Moses, my master, make them stop!" But Moses replied, "Are you jealous for my sake? I wish that all the LORD's people were prophets and that the LORD would put his Spirit upon them all!"
> —NUMBERS 11:26–29

Moses lovingly rebuked Joshua for his overly zealous loyalty. I love that! Every leader should take this view. Yet what we see too often looks more like dictatorship than servanthood. Granted, *dictatorship* is a strong word; it refers to "a style of leadership where there is always personal control over the decision-making process for the team."[1] Dictatorial leaders tend to make decisions that are based on their own moral codes. Politically speaking, "a dictatorship is formed when a specific group seizes power, with the composition of this group affecting how power is seized and how the eventual dictatorship will rule."[2]

These insights about dictatorship mirror what is happening in many legalistic cult-type churches. Only on rare occasions have I met an ultra-religious pastor who was deeply humble (and it usually happened when a pastor was breaking away from legalism). In most cases the church leader is seen as a Moses-type figure with whom God is believed to speak directly. Therefore, the church is expected to follow with blind obedience or face the consequences.

This dictatorship leadership style is somewhat milder and harder to detect than the cult leadership of people like Jim Jones and David Koresh. This milder form is hidden in the office rather than the person. The consideration for office also existed in Jesus' day. The Pharisees never demanded that the people worship them, but they did abuse the office they held. Jesus described their office, saying, "The scribes and the Pharisees sit in Moses' seat" (Matt. 23:2, kjv).

The seat is a place of authority, like the judge's seat in a courtroom. The scribes and Pharisees were fixated on the idea of sitting in Moses's seat and wielding the executive power Moses had, spiritually speaking. While Jesus acknowledged the Pharisees' position, He also took issue with them, saying, "Practice and obey whatever they [the Pharisees] tell you, but don't follow their example. For they don't practice what they teach. They crush people with unbearable religious demands and never lift a finger to ease the burden" (Matt. 23:3–4).

Some church leaders have lost the fear of the Lord and are abusing their authority by enforcing legalistic rules that burden the people with sadness and an inability to be joyful. I have seen leaders abuse their God-given authority by having members carry them to the pulpit in chariots! Other pastors have their musicians play jubilant music as they (the pastors) ascend to their pulpits.

In my early days as a guest speaker I attended dinner with a host church's pastor and some of his entourage. None of them spoke, and starting a conversation with them was impossible. Something similar happened when my wife and I (as guest speakers) were assigned "armor-bearers" who were forbidden to talk to us. When I broke protocol and made our armor-bearers laugh, they suffered repercussions. Later on I saw the church's head administrator scolding them for dishonoring the rules. My heart broke! When I asked them if they were OK, they said they could not speak to us, but they were grateful to my wife and me for being friendly toward them.

Are you wondering how veneration produces such incredible control over time? Ahead are some clues from the story of Moses and the children of Israel.

Moses heard from God

Moses's relationship with God was profound and profoundly different from the norm, beginning with the fact that Moses absolutely heard from God. The people were so certain of this that they asked to hear not from God directly but only through Moses.

> When the people heard the thunder and the loud blast of the ram's horn, and when they saw the flashes of lightning and the smoke billowing from the mountain, they stood at a distance, trembling with fear. And they said to Moses, "You speak to us, and we will listen. But don't let God speak directly to us, or we will die!"
> —Exodus 20:18–19

This is where I believe the fear of God was replaced by the fear of God's man. If you keep reading the story, Moses tried to stop the people from taking this route, but they kept moving toward their extreme honor and veneration of him. Today, many pastors, bishops, apostles, and prophets fail to rebuke this level of loyalty and allow themselves to be placed on higher pedestals than God intended for them. Should such men and women of God ever fall from grace, those who idolized them are likely to fall too.

During Jesus' time, the Jews were still so committed to Moses that I personally believe it detracted from their love of God and their ability to accept Jesus. Yes, they loved God, but they also loved God's man. They even said, "We know God spoke to Moses, but we don't even know where this man [Jesus] comes from" (John 9:29).

They were absolutely (and correctly) convinced that God spoke to Moses. This is where I think their slide into an excessive form of veneration began. In all fairness, many leaders who become dictatorial don't start out that way. But because God speaks to them, their followers tend to deify them. Their idea of leading God's people eventually becomes corrupted with pride, control, and money, and they cross lines they probably never thought they would cross.

Moses gave them manna

If knowing that God spoke to His people through Moses caused them to venerate him, imagine how receiving manna from heaven affected them. Every day for forty years, the manna appeared, and the Israelites ate it. God supernaturally fed His people as a type and shadow of faithful followers of Christ receiving revelation that other people don't receive. Jesus acknowledged the manna but corrected the Jews' perception of who provided it.

> [The crowd said to Jesus,] "After all, our ancestors ate manna while they journeyed through the wilderness! The Scriptures say, 'Moses gave them bread from heaven to eat.'" Jesus said, "I tell you the truth, Moses didn't give you bread from heaven. My Father did. And now he offers you the true bread from heaven. The true bread of God is the one who comes down from heaven and gives life to the world."
> —JOHN 6:31–33

The nation of Israel remained grateful to Moses for the manna and for his role in hearing from God. People today are so grateful for the revelation they are receiving from the Bible—things they never heard before. It makes them feel special and creates a special connection to the leader whom they see as the provider of this revelation (manna). Therefore, they offer their leader extreme honor that sometimes becomes inappropriate.

Many years ago I was under the covering of such a leader. I was so blown away by the revelations I was receiving that I became blind to the control this person had over me. I believed this leader could do no wrong. Whatever he taught was coming directly from the Holy Spirit as far as I was concerned. I eventually learned that much of what he presented in his teachings he had plagiarized from other anointed teachers. But for a significant period of time, my loyalty was like that of Israel toward Moses.

This person told our church we were only to receive teaching directly from him, and we obeyed. When people tried to tell me I was becoming cult minded, I fiercely rebuked them. I was like Peter cutting off the ear of Malchus. My devotion made me a zealot for this leader, and no one was going to change that.

I thank God that He opened my eyes! That's when my family and I ran for our lives. This is the reason I am so vocal about this issue. I stand against false apostles and prophets because I was blinded by one. Moses was not a false prophet. Even so, the people's allegiance to him blinded them to the ultimate Prophet when He stood right in front of them.

A Tabernacle for Moses

As staunch disciples of Moses, the children of Israel wanted to know where their teacher lived. In Old Testament times this was a way of establishing personal intimacy. When the disciples of John the Baptist left to follow Jesus, they had the same desire. "John's two disciples...followed Jesus. Jesus looked around and saw them following. 'What do you want?' he asked them. They replied, 'Rabbi' (which means 'Teacher'), 'where are you staying?'" (John 1:37–38).

The idea of tabernacle also established intimacy. When Jesus appeared on the Mount of Transfiguration, Moses and Elijah appeared with Jesus. Seeing this, "Peter...said unto Jesus, Lord, it is good for us to be here: if thou wilt, let us make here three tabernacles; one for thee, and one for Moses, and one for [Elijah]" (Matt. 17:4, KJV).

Peter's intentions were good, but our heavenly Father corrected him, telling him and the other disciples who were present that although Moses and Elijah were standing with Jesus, the disciples were to hear only Jesus. How I wish everyone trapped in legalistic and spiritually abusive environments would embrace this message! Even if they are hearing Jesus, many have built tabernacles for their earthly leaders. They are setting up tents beside Jesus, but they are trying to follow "Jesus + Moses" or "Jesus + Elijah." Either equation adds up to a false gospel!

Mark's Gospel makes an interesting statement about Peter's offer to build three tabernacles: "He said this because he didn't really know what else to say, for they were all terrified" (Mark 9:6). I hate to say this, but most believers who venerate their leaders or churches have no idea why they're doing it. Some custom or tradition was passed down to them, and they blindly follow it.

When my eyes opened to this reality in my own life, I saw that I had built a tabernacle for my spiritual leader right beside Jesus, and I started asking unwelcome questions. I wanted to know how such loyalty takes people beyond what is scripturally sound. If your church or leader doesn't allow questions about dogma, views, or traditions, or discourages members from engaging in critical thinking, then you are being spiritually abused.

To give you an idea of how high on a pedestal I held my leaders (especially my pastor), I allowed them to steer me away from things I knew for sure God had prompted me to do. If they nixed whatever it was, I abandoned the idea and assumed I had missed God or was being emotional. When I came out of legalism, the Holy Spirit convicted me of all the times I disobeyed Him in the name of submitting to my pastor. I wept so hard to think that I had been so deceived! I had been taught that whatever the pastor says is the voice of God—period. But my theology in this was not biblical.

If you see yourself in my story or in Peter's heartfelt but misplaced desire to build tabernacles, go ahead and repent right now. Ask the Lord to forgive your ignorance. He loves you and has been waiting all these years for you to lay down your unhealthy view of your pastor.

Accusation: The Culture of Moses

Honoring your pastor with a pure heart is beneficial, but when the idea gets distorted, it presents a darker side, which is a culture of accusation. In legalistic environments that place an overly high value on honoring men and women of God, accusation is a strong force. In some cases the people seem to honor their leader more than Jesus. Everything they do seems to be centered around pleasing the leader. But when they don't perform perfectly, accusations fly in their direction. Of course, everyone fails to measure up at some point, and everyone is eventually accused of wrongdoing.

This type of culture is exactly what Jesus dealt with when He dialogued with the people. He told them their negative attitude toward Him formed because they were constantly under accusation by the Law of Moses, and even Moses himself. Jesus said, "It isn't I who will accuse you before the Father. *Moses will accuse you!* Yes, Moses, in whom you put your hopes" (John 5:45, emphasis added).

This must have struck a chord in the people. Jesus showed them how extreme and futile their veneration of Moses was. He warned them that they would always fall short under the Law of Moses, regardless of their allegiance to him. This idea has application in today's spiritually abusive churches. People who serve their leaders with blind loyalty are met with accusation the moment they ask the slightest question or have a second thought. After years of faithful service and after giving so much of their time, money, and energy to the church, these people are cut off as though they never existed. Often, they are blacklisted and blackballed by the leader they served.

I sense that someone reading this is weeping because they were faithful to the "man or woman of God" but received only banishment in the end. Is that you? If so, I've been where you are. The covering I was under promised "the inheritance" to all faithful sons and daughters of the ministry. That promise mattered so much that when every discernment alarm fired in my soul and I lost faith in my leader, I told my wife (for years), "I don't care. I just want my inheritance."

You can probably guess—the only inheritance I received was heartache and pain. This leader and I had a huge falling out and went our separate ways. All the time and energy I invested seemed to count for nothing. I got tired of this person continually calling with accusations about everybody, including me. It wore out my soul until I finally snapped and told the person that I was leaving.

It was the best move I could have made. As soon as I left, the healing started. If you are where I was, leave that legalistic church. It's killing you and your family, and spiritual abuse is 100 percent unacceptable. Don't be afraid. The Lord will protect you, much as He protected me. Within a year of walking away from that leader, our ministry exploded globally. We became leading voices for deliverance, started writing best-selling books, were featured in Christian motion pictures, and planted multiple churches. My former covering would not have allowed that level of success because they believed that "a son can never be greater than his father," just as Abraham can never be greater than Melchizedek.

Speaking of Melchizedek: False Doctrine

This is a good time to mention a certain false doctrine. It involves modern-day apostles and prophets who consider themselves as types of Melchizedek to their churches, ministries, and movements. Based on this philosophy, their spiritual sons and daughters must give special tithes directly to them, just as Abraham (then Abram) did with Melchizedek in Genesis 14.

These leaders carry themselves in a kingly or priestly manner that would seem fitting for Melchizedek, and they expect the people under their covering to view them the same way. Within the church such teachings about the order of Melchizedek are distortions of the truth. Abram gave his spoils of war to Melchizedek, and Melchizedek gave Abram a blessing. This is a biblical reality. But this idea is playing out in unhealthy ways, largely within the African American and Latino churches, where the absence of father figures is prominent.

Regardless of the extreme sacrifices people make in such churches, the worth of the faithful is measured by how much they give to, submit to, publicly thank, and defend their leader, their

Melchizedek. Some pastors even require additional giving in the form of a *terumah* offering, which was established in Judaism as a form of priestly dues along the lines of Abram's offering to Melchizedek.[3] But there is a problem with the *terumah* in the church: Your pastor is not your Melchizedek; Jesus is! Stop giving all your hard-earned money to these charlatans, and run for your life.

Don't believe the lie that leaving will remove "their anointing" from you. They are not priests "in the order of Melchizedek" (Heb. 5:10). The anointing isn't theirs anyway. I remember when I told my former covering I was leaving. The response was, "If you leave me, I will pull the anointing off your life." But the anointing wasn't his to give or take away.

Leave any movement that holds to this Melchizedek doctrine. It is a moneymaking scheme that allows leaders to live lavishly. This is not the heart of Christ but a form of spiritual abuse that manipulates people into ungodly submission. Jesus, our great High Priest, is not like this. He said, "The rulers in this world lord it over their people, and officials flaunt their authority over those under them. But among you it will be different. Whoever wants to be a leader among you must be your servant" (Matt. 20:25–26).

THE MOMMA OF THE HOUSE

The spiritual abuse I have described so far extends beyond male figureheads in churches and organizations. Many spiritual abusers also demand extra loyalty to their wives as the "mommas" of the house or movement. Don't misunderstand me: There is nothing wrong with calling the pastor's wife *Momma*. There is something wrong with spiritual sons and daughters being required to wait on the mommas hand and foot.

I've seen this play out with followers waiting outside "Momma's office," ready to carry her bag and her water and even wipe the sweat from her brow. My wife witnessed an armor-bearer scratching an itch for a pastor's wife. I am not exaggerating; my wife saw this with her own eyes!

In many churches where a legitimate fear exists among the members concerning the momma of the house, you hear the saying, "My momma don't play." This is common where the pastor's wife is lording over God's flock. Like all abuses, the idea of honor to the momma of the house is cultish and diabolical. We should cherish the pastor's wife but not idolize or fear her. She is required by God to serve God's people. God does not require the church to serve her. Giving her the title of queen and requiring spiritual sons and daughters to give her numerous monetary gifts (the birthday seed, Christmas seed, Mother's Day seed, and Pastor's Day seed) go too far. And some churches go even further.

I hesitated about writing this chapter because so much of it seems unbelievable. I'm not surprised if you find it hard to take these accounts at face value. However, this kind of spiritual abuse really exists, and saying nothing is not a viable option.

Mosaic Patterns and Stagnation

I once met a pastor who dressed like a Hasidic Jew (excluding the Russian hat). He wore black and patterned his ministry around a mildly Hebraic system of worship. I never understood why he did this, and it always seemed cultish to me. I got to know this minister indirectly, through his children, who were connected with our ministry. I was convinced he loved God with all his heart and was truly born again. But he maintained an affinity for Old Testament worship, albeit with a Messianic flavor.

Although I still believe this man is truly saved, I noticed a pattern of ministry dysfunction that never seemed to be resolved. The church remained small, ranging from somewhere below sixty members to as many as one hundred. The church lacked structure and was short of capable staffing. The administrative elders were the pastor's wife and children, along with some older women. Financial resources were in short supply, and the church building was always a storefront.

In time, even the pastor's children left the ministry to become leaders in more vibrant churches. I have concluded that this man's patterning his ministry more after Moses than after Jesus was the cause of the ministry's stagnation. Moses is one of the great servants in our heritage, but Jesus said in John 12:32, "When I am lifted up from the earth, I will draw everyone to myself." We are to look "unto Jesus the author and finisher of our faith" (Heb. 12:2, KJV).

BREAKING FREE AND MOVING FORWARD

Jesus deserves more honor than Moses

How can an overemphasized view of Moses be solved? By turning the focus back to Jesus! Jesus has more glory (ascribed value) than Moses. When the value of something goes up, the Bible calls it glory! Hebrews 3:3 says, "Jesus deserves far more glory than Moses, just as a person who builds a house deserves more praise than the house itself."

Intellectually, you might know this, but you might still pattern yourself using Old Testament identity markers, which we will discuss later on. Legalistic churches often give Jesus less glory than He deserves. At a deep level they pattern themselves after a Mosaic model, becoming more like the tabernacle of Moses than like a true Christian church. Some churches leave you thinking of the tabernacle in the wilderness or the temple of Solomon. Some churches are named "Mount Sinai," "Tabernacle of Testimony," or "Pillar of Fire." These names point not to Jesus but to Moses. My point is not to be critical but to make an honest observation and offer insight.

God is speaking through Jesus

What God is saying is very much linked to the person through whom He is saying it.

> Long ago God spoke many times and in many ways to our ancestors through the prophets. And now in these final days, he has spoken to us through his Son. God promised everything to the Son as an inheritance, and through the Son he created the universe.
> —HEBREWS 1:1–2

This passage poses a threat to religious dogma that is centered around Moses and other figures. Everything must center around Jesus because He is the One speaking—not Elijah, not Moses, not Enoch, not John the Baptist, Paul, Peter, David, Solomon, or anybody else. God is speaking to His church *only* through Jesus, and the Holy Spirit is saying only what Jesus is saying.

Let the following texts sink in:

> When he, the Spirit of truth, is come, he will guide you into all truth: for he shall not speak of himself; but whatsoever he shall hear, that shall he speak, and he will shew you things to come. He shall glorify me [Jesus]: for he shall receive of mine, and shall shew it unto you.
> —JOHN 16:13–14, KJV

> But the Comforter, which is the Holy Ghost, whom the Father will send in my name, he shall teach you all things, and bring all things to your remembrance, whatsoever I [Jesus] have said unto you.
> —JOHN 14:26, KJV

> But when the Father sends the Advocate as my representative—that is, the Holy Spirit—he will teach you everything and will remind you of everything I [Jesus] have told you.
> —JOHN 14:26

The Holy Spirit testifies of Jesus and not your leader, pastor, bishop, apostle, or spiritual father or mother. It's all about Christ, and your extreme submission should be toward Him alone. I'm not saying you shouldn't submit to your leadership; I am saying to stay away from extreme submission to your leadership. Don't substitute church leaders for Jesus. Don't give them what is His!

God is molding us to be like Jesus

The apostle Paul was clear about detoxing from legalism and coming into Christ. He did it by showing us God's overall objective toward our being conformed to the image of His Son. God is not conforming us to any other biblical personality or earthly figure. "Whom he did foreknow, he also did predestinate to be conformed to the image of his Son, that he might be the firstborn among many brethren" (Rom. 8:29, KJV).

From before the foundation of the world, God purposed to conform us to His Son. My spirit leaps as I type these words! Our heavenly Father is personally invested in making sure that, in the end, we look like Jesus. And when He sees us, He sees Jesus. When we speak, we sound like Jesus. When we love, we love like Jesus. Hallelujah!

And on top of that He has given us the mind (not of Moses but) of Christ! "For, 'Who can know the LORD's thoughts? Who knows enough to teach him?' But we understand these things, for we have the mind of Christ" (1 Cor. 2:16).

Paul's focus should be our focus

The apostle Paul let us know that for the sake of pursuing Christ and the gospel of grace (not legalism and not the gospel with a touch of legalism), he counted as worthless everything he learned under the Mosaic system. Let the following words become your own:

> Yea doubtless, and I count all things but loss for the excellency of the knowledge of Christ Jesus my Lord: for whom I have suffered the loss of all things, and do count them but dung, that I may win Christ.
>
> —PHILIPPIANS 3:8, KJV

Chapter 7

OVEREMPHASIS ON APPEARANCE

Gideon made a sacred ephod from the gold and put it in Ophrah, his hometown. But soon all the Israelites prostituted themselves by worshiping it, and it became a trap for Gideon and his family.
—Judges 8:27

BE FOREWARNED: This chapter will cause controversy for some readers. This is because in legalistic churches the dogma regarding attire has been more divisive than almost any issue other than music. Yet God's own words to Samuel, who was seeking God's successor to King Saul, destroy the controversy:

> Do not look on his appearance or on the height of his stature, because I have rejected him. For the Lord sees not as man sees: man looks on the outward appearance, but the Lord looks on the heart.
> —1 Samuel 16:7, esv

The Lord declared plainly that He does not judge our outward appearance. Yet so many churches and denominations still claim to know people's hearts by how they dress. Why are they trying to do the work of the Holy Spirit? And why do they ignore God's real concern with the inner disposition of a person's heart?

Discerning God's Heart on Dress

Before we search out the issue of man's attempts to manage God's intent where appearance is concerned, an important point must be made: God is not entirely silent about what we wear. He indeed established at least two rules concerning dress. The first one involves gender; the second involves modesty:

> » "A woman must not put on men's clothing, and a man must not wear women's clothing. Anyone who does this is detestable in the sight of the Lord your God" (Deut. 22:5).

> » "Women should adorn themselves in respectable apparel, with modesty and self-control" (1 Tim. 2:9, ESV).

More on this later. For now, my question for you is simple: Do you really believe the Father, who sent His Son to save sinners from hell, would then send them to the lake of fire because of clothing? The rules God mentioned above show that God is looking not for damnation but distinction, which involves "perceiving someone or something as being not the same and often treating as separate or different."[1] The law regarding dress codes is about differentiating between male and female and between modesty and immodesty. The law wasn't meant to enslave God's people. Nor did it impose a standard by which human beings could rightfully judge one another's spirituality.

Distinction implies separation. So by commanding His people to dress modestly, God emphasized their separation from the world's excesses. When churches take this idea to extremes, the result is a cultlike, appearance-based Christianity that corrupts modesty and turns distinction into extinction! The church doesn't grow because the preoccupation with externals causes so many people to leave and discourages so many others from taking part in the first place.

During a midweek prayer service in the first church I pastored,

I saw one of our faithful members standing outside our building and peeking inside. When I beckoned to her from the pulpit, she motioned back that she would not come inside because of her outfit. She had come from work and was wearing her hospital scrubs, which included pants. It took a while to convince her that it was OK to join us in prayer, and when she did, God touched her powerfully.

You might be thinking I should have honored the woman's conviction about what she had been taught. But what she learned was suspect. And leaving her outside feeling rejected while we continued to pray and get blessed seems unlike anything Jesus would do. When God gave the children of Israel a dress code, fanatic judgmentalism was not His intent; a degree of separation from the debauchery of societal norms was.

The New Testament also speaks about how we dress. Certain texts speak in detail on the subject. Both Paul and Peter—two apostles with different perspectives and different assignments—weigh in on the issue. Although their positions overlap, they are very different. Understanding each man's perspective helps us discern the intent.

But first, I want to stress an important point that captures God's larger perspective. Paul wrote, "All of you who were baptized into Christ have clothed yourselves with Christ. There is neither Jew nor Gentile, neither slave nor free, *nor is there male and female*, for you are all one in Christ Jesus" (Gal. 3:27–28, NIV, emphasis added).

Paul makes it clear that both men and women are called to God's standards of holiness. However, the church places a much greater and harsher emphasis on how women dress. This is important to note because women have encountered a bias in this area, and I don't want to perpetuate it. So let's examine the apostles' instructions while keeping cultural contexts in mind.

Apostle Paul's dress code

Let's revisit Paul's writings to Timothy and go a little further into his mention of our outward appearance.

> Women should adorn themselves in respectable apparel, with modesty and self-control, not with braided hair and gold or pearls or costly attire, but with what is proper for women who profess godliness—with good works.
> —1 Timothy 2:9–10, ESV

Notice Paul stated some prohibitions for women, not to control them but to encourage them to testify well through their appearance. One word in the passage sticks out: The word is *adorn*, and its definition illuminates what Paul is saying. To *adorn* is "to enhance the appearance of especially with beautiful objects."[2] This definition changes things! Where legalistic dress codes are taught, the idea seems to be that God wants His people to look poor (which is not to say that God desires us to flaunt riches). Paul talks about women adorning themselves but doing it respectably. Clothing can be expensive or inexpensive, as long as it conveys respectability.

Obviously, the word *respectable* needs to be understood. It means "decent or correct in character or behavior."[3] As Christians we are to dress in a way that expresses Christlike character and behavior. When I first visited churches, men couldn't wear tank tops. Godly men even had to wear full shirts during workouts in their local gym. However, what you wear is only part of the equation. How and why you wear it is another. If a gentleman hopes to seduce women by wearing a tight tank top, his intentions and dress are not respectable because his behavior is not Christlike. The issue is not his shirt but his heart.

The apostle Paul addressed not only clothing but how Christians are to conduct themselves. If they act modestly and possess self-control, they won't need church leadership pushing dress codes down their throats. The people's own modesty and self-control will govern their apparel choices. So let's talk more about these traits and also about the profession of godliness.

Modesty

Modesty is "propriety in dress, speech, or conduct."[4] *Propriety* is "conformity to what is socially acceptable" or inoffensive.[5] When we adorn ourselves with modesty, we are mindful not to offend the cause of Christ by our choice of attire. Some Christian denominations are so extreme, however, that their followers dress in apparel from the eighteenth century. Physically, it suggests modesty and seems pious, but it stirs offense. Why? Because we're in the twenty-first century, and there are plenty of respectable clothing choices currently available.

I'm not suggesting we shun groups such as the Amish, Mennonites, Quakers, and others. But these movements are declining, with perhaps their only growth coming from births within their families. While they focus their attention on rules and regulations, they are rapidly losing their influence in evangelism and are not focused on winning the lost.

Self-control

In the passage from 1 Timothy chapter 2 Paul also mentioned self-control, a fruit of the Spirit that empowers the believer to live righteously, pray faithfully, and walk according to God's Word. We are not left to fend for ourselves—not even when it comes to choosing what we wear. The Spirit will convict us or approve our attire. We don't have to ask, "What would You like me to wear today?" We choose what to wear by making choices and sensing the witness of the Spirit.

Ephesians 4:30 says, "Grieve not the holy Spirit of God, whereby ye are sealed unto the day of redemption" (KJV). When believers try to force the issue of what to wear, they are attempting to take the Holy Spirit's place, which grieves Him. Creating lists of rules and regulations is a way of saying the Spirit's power isn't strong enough to keep us walking in the fruit of self-control. But following legalistic rules is not what it means to be led by the Spirit. Paul rebuked the Galatians for this very thing, writing, "How foolish can you be?

After starting your new lives in the Spirit, why are you now trying to become perfect by your own human effort?" (Gal. 3:3).

It saddens me to see so many believers trying to help the Holy Spirit. Listen, if the Spirit is within you and has sealed you, rejoice! Jesus has sent the Comforter, your Advocate, to help you. (See John 14:16.) Fear not. Just trust the Lord for your sanctification. He's got you covered.

Godliness

Bearing in mind God's desire for a distinction between His people and the rest of the world, we can ask, "How far should that distinction go, and where do we draw the line?" I believe the answer is in 1 Timothy 2:10, where Paul mentioned those who "profess godliness" (ESV).

The vocabulary got my attention; the word *professional* comes from the word *profess*. You could say that as believers we are to be professional in our expression of godliness. That eliminates the idea of using our liberty to bend the rules concerning biblical holiness. But Paul also said a Christian's professional expression of godliness would be evident in our good works!

Apostle Peter's approach to appearance

Now for the viewpoint of the apostle Peter, which was very different from Paul's. Peter didn't address clothing and other external adornments, as Paul did. Instead, he spoke about the inner man. The two apostles' perspectives certainly overlap, but the uniqueness of their respective views is clear from Peter's first epistle:

> Do not let your adorning be external—the braiding of hair and the putting on of gold jewelry, or the clothing you wear—but let your adorning be the hidden person of the heart with the imperishable beauty of a gentle and quiet spirit, which in God's sight is very precious.
> —1 Peter 3:3–4, ESV

Wow! Peter said not to be preoccupied with attire but to focus on character development. A *preoccupation* is "the state of being worried about or thinking about something most of the time."[6] As a fisher of men Peter was not about to be distracted by trivial matters such as clothing. I also believe he wanted to keep Christians from being "choked by the cares...of life" (Luke 8:14, ESV). It is easy to see how an extreme focus on attire leans toward vanity, not only in women but in men.

It might seem that Peter's focus on the internal is contradictory to Paul's external approach to dress, but it's not. In fact, these two perspectives complement each other. If we embrace what both apostles wrote, we discover that true biblical sanctification (in regard to dress codes and other matters) is not legalistic or hard. It is a matter of being freely led by the Spirit.

Let's look now on the gentle and quiet spirit Peter emphasized.

Gentle spirit

I absolutely love that Peter presented gentleness as he did, because gentleness is a fruit of the Spirit. Just as self-control is needed in external beauty, gentleness is an element of inner beauty. However, this gentle inner behavior produces a public witness. And in relation to attire, gentleness positively affects a believer's dress. Without it the wrong clothing would seem appropriate to wear.

Peter explained that if your soul is gentle, gentleness is displayed outwardly as sanctification that bears witness to your true discipleship in Christ. Because of your gentleness, you more easily depend on the Holy Spirit to guide you. You are not religious or aggressive about looking right. You do not distract from Christ but lean in to Him and reflect Him from within and without. For all these reasons Peter urged us to depend on the Holy Spirit and the fruit of gentleness.

Quiet spirit

The byproduct of gentleness is expressed with a quiet spirit, but what does quietness have to do with attire? The answer is *everything*.

Clothing and appearance can be aggressive and loud, and therefore distracting. The prophet Isaiah had something to say about loud clothing:

> The LORD says, "The women of Zion are haughty, walking along with outstretched necks, flirting with their eyes, strutting along with swaying hips, with ornaments jingling on their ankles. Therefore the LORD will bring sores on the heads of the women of Zion; the LORD will make their scalps bald."
> —ISAIAH 3:16–17, NIV

Again, I emphasize that God is referring to anyone who is seductive, not only females. Men can wear clothing that sends out the wrong message (especially in church). But the quietness that Peter talked about does the opposite. Having a quietness in one's personality and allowing gentleness to reign in one's heart causes external changes, including changes in knowing how to dress. It's not about extreme measures, rules, and fears of wearing the wrong thing. Peter carefully stressed allowing the Holy Spirit to shift your focus from the external appearance and redirect it to what God truly intended, which is an inward Christlike state.

LEGALISM'S LINGERING LIES

When my wife and I were newly married and thinking about having children, I mentioned that if we had a little girl, I would buy her some pretty earrings. My wife immediately protested that earrings were sinful and "not from God."

I honestly didn't know how to answer her, so I said in anger, "Well, I'm going to buy *my* daughter earrings!"

When I asked my wife to explain her reaction, she shared a bizarre teaching about how Jezebel wore jewelry and makeup to disguise herself before Jehu. According to this teaching, wearing makeup and jewelry meant you were imitating Jezebel. In addition, because owned livestock had their ears pierced in Old Testament times, piercing your ears was the same as saying you were livestock. This belief was so ingrained in my wife's thinking that when she tried to rebel and buy earrings, her earlobes swelled!

At some point, I left the subject alone. But months later I bought my wife some diamond earrings for her birthday. When she saw my gift, she protested and worried that her ears would swell again. I looked at her and said, "That's legalism. You're free in Christ, and I know when you put these on, you will not swell up. You'll look pretty to me."

She finally agreed to wear them. Her ears didn't swell, and she's worn earrings ever since. She never needed jewelry to look beautiful because she's naturally beautiful. But seeing her break out of an extreme view was a matter of principle, and it was wonderful. As for "my" daughter wearing earrings, God in His humor gave us two boys!

I share these stories as a slice of real life that many people face each day. A pastor friend of mine mentioned his denomination became extreme concerning external appearance and banned the wearing of any kind of jewelry, including wedding rings. That year, a new overseer was selected, and when the denomination had their annual national convocation, the event was jam-packed with an unusual number of women from around the country.

When my pastor friend asked why there was such an influx of women, he learned they flocked to see what the overseer's wife was wearing. They knew if she wore something, they could wear it too. Well, the new overseer's wife wore earrings and other jewelry. The following day, all the women wore them too!

People might tolerate legalism for a variety of reasons, but they long to be free.

Breaking Free and Moving Forward

Convictions can be wrong

Remember the story of the woman in her hospital scrubs. She believed she was unwelcome in the prayer meeting because she was wearing pants. I invited her in because any sense of conviction she felt over her scrubs was based not in biblical truth but in the legalistic training she had received. What she believed was misleading and manipulating her!

It's so important to remember that our convictions can mislead us. Having a personal conviction, even if you feel it very strongly, does not mean it is from God. The Holy Spirit convicts us "concerning sin and righteousness and judgment" (John 16:8, ESV), but people and systems that condemn us are not doing so by way of the Holy Spirit.

Our views and other people's views can be exaggerated and become stumbling blocks. That's why Paul wrote, "Let not then your good be evil spoken of" (Rom. 14:16, KJV).

Freedom is a process

Page by page and day by day, let the Holy Spirit detox you from excessive concerns over external appearances that distract you from the more important disposition of your inner heart and intent. As you shed any remaining legalistic bonds through God's presence and your growing intimacy with Him, true biblical modesty and holiness will be your portion—not by your efforts but by resting in Him and allowing Him to penetrate any area that is keeping you entangled in rules, dress codes, or condemnation.

God is leading you somewhere, and He needs your undivided attention. Keep your eyes on Him, and watch all legalistic distractions fall away. Enjoy the experience of seeing through His eyes more and more and feeling the burden of legalism less and less. Watch the old struggles over what you should or should not wear melt away, and enjoy a newfound simplicity in making wardrobe choices.

Now that you have a clearer sense of Jesus' heart in regard to clothing, I strongly encourage you to ask the Holy Spirit to break your mind free concerning this topic. Please pray this prayer aloud:

> *Holy Spirit, I thank You for giving me revelation concerning Your true intention for Your people regarding external sanctification. I ask that You set me free from the legalism that has me trying to please You through human effort. Lord, I ask that self-control and gentleness be in my life right now by Your Spirit so that I can walk worthy of the vocation to which You called me. Lord Jesus, I give You my mind; please give me the mind of Christ so that I can represent You in everything, especially in my attire. In Jesus' name, amen.*

Chapter 8

RESISTANCE TO CHANGE

Their minds are full of darkness; they wander far from the life God gives because they have closed their minds and hardened their hearts against him.
—Ephesians 4:18

It's easy to get frustrated with people "who don't know." I used to do that a lot, and when people ignore or don't recognize extreme legalism, I still get frustrated at times. But as my wife always says, "You can't get mad at them if all they know is all they know."

It's a mic drop moment every time Ibelize says that! Why? Because the statement is true. People who don't know what they don't know aren't typically rejecting knowledge; they simply lack it. Hosea 4:6 deals with this issue. The second part of the verse warns against rejecting knowledge; but the first part points to the devastation that comes from lacking knowledge, whatever the cause. It says, "My people are destroyed for lack of knowledge" (Hos. 4:6, KJV).

Throughout this book we have explored the effects of legalism, one of which is spiritual blindness. The Bible speaks of the veil obscuring people's vision. But sometimes we become so familiar with the veil that we cling to and even worship it. Amazingly, according to Acts 17:30, there was a time when "God winked" at ignorance (KJV), meaning He offered a measure of grace to those who didn't know or hadn't been taught to understand certain truths. The verse goes on to say, "But now he commands everyone everywhere to repent of their sins and turn to him" (Acts 17:30).

No one is entirely unaccountable for their ignorance, but I believe it's safe to say that in His justice God will not fault those who never had the opportunity to discover their ignorance. It took me years to realize I wasn't always ignorant on purpose—and neither are you. When Peter preached in the temple, he attributed the hostility of Jewish leaders to a lack of knowledge, saying, "Friends, I realize that what you and your leaders did to Jesus was done in ignorance" (Acts 3:17).

Information (and its lack) shapes worldviews, and worldviews determine actions. The high priest thought killing Jesus was the right thing to do. Saul of Tarsus thought killing Christians was a righteous act. Years after his conversion, he wrote, "Being ignorant of the righteousness of God, and seeking to establish their own, they did not submit to God's righteousness" (Rom. 10:3, ESV). Paul was pointing out how his fellow Jewish leaders were in the same kind of ignorance that once blinded him. They simply didn't know what they didn't know! So while ignorance can be dangerous and keep a person from walking in their full freedom in Christ, God recognizes when someone is unintentionally unaware.

Having said all that, ignorance is not an excuse! There comes a time when God requires us to embrace truths that upgrade our understanding. I look back over thirty years in the gospel and see how much my theology has changed. The core of my Christian orthodoxy remains intact, but my secondary doctrines have evolved, and I have abandoned some. Doctrines for which I once would have fought now leave me saying in all prayerfulness, "Wow, Lord, I did not realize that!"

Life is a learning curve! We all are growing in our knowledge of the Scriptures, and as we do, our behavior gets adjusted accordingly (or should). Whether we completely understand a certain matter or not, we need to remain teachable and not resist God. Let's always be willing to flow with the stream of revelation He opens to us from Scripture.

LEGALISM PRODUCES STUBBORNNESS

Throughout Old Testament scriptures and through early church history we find examples of stubborn belief systems and people who refused to change. These cases prove you can love the Lord and live a consecrated lifestyle but be as stubborn as a mule. Even as you receive sound insight, you can cling to an old, misguided idea.

To fight our stubbornness and ignorance, we Christians are called not only to follow God's Word but also to hear His voice. Jesus said, "My sheep hear my voice, and I know them, and they follow me" (John 10:27, KJV). The Christian life depends on (1) the sufficiency of Scripture, (2) learning to discern Jesus' voice in Scripture, and (3) following Him wherever He leads. The Great Shepherd regularly leads us sheep to eat new grass in unfamiliar meadows. This is how He takes us from glory to glory and faith to faith.

However, we undermine this pattern of growth when we prefer our ignorance to change. The Bible often calls spiritually stubborn people *stiff-necked*. In every believer there is some rigidity and a propensity to resist change, no matter how beneficial the change might be. The children of Israel were notorious in this regard, particularly where the Law of Moses was concerned. They were heavily invested in the Law, and they were downright stubborn about clinging to it.

I believe this explains Jesus' frequent expression, "But I say unto you." It was a signal that He was introducing a kind of upgrade to their understanding—information they would consider to be new. They had a problem receiving the upgrade. Because they had dwelled so long in what they had learned, they resisted anything that seemed to bring their understanding into question. The Law of

Moses was all they ever knew. So they resisted change, even when the Messiah they had waited for so long personally delivered it!

Israel's resistance to change was largely due to their training and the rules that guided every aspect of their lives. They were certain they knew all there was to know about how their religion worked. But Jesus sought to reveal things that had been hidden behind the veil. The Greek word for *revelation* is *apokalupsis*, and it is all about an "unveiling, disclosure....uncovering."[1] Jesus wanted to unveil some things to God's people!

If revelation is an unveiling, ignorance is a veiling. The extensive metaphorical use of the word *veil* in Scripture provides volumes of insight. When a person is ignorant, it is as though a veil has been draped over their mind. Our particular interest is in how the word *veil* relates to legalism, but veils always work the same way. You can preach and teach to someone that legalism contradicts the gospel until you're blue in the face, but unless the Lord removes the veil, your attempts will prove feeble.

The Veil, Physically and Spiritually

Understanding the purpose of the veil under the Old Testament helps us connect the dots for the rest of this chapter. In the simplest way, the word *veil* indicates a head covering—a cloth used to conceal the face or protect the head from outside influences. As the centuries passed, the veil took on a deeper meaning, becoming part of many cultural customs and religions. Therefore, we see head coverings in the Old and New Testaments, especially regarding women and marriage. Paul also explained the connection between veils and headship:

> The head of every man is Christ, the head of woman is man, and the head of Christ is God. A man dishonors his head if he covers his head while praying or prophesying. But a woman dishonors her head if she prays or prophesies without a covering on her head, for this is the same as shaving her head.

> Yes, if she refuses to wear a head covering, she should cut off all her hair! But since it is shameful for a woman to have her hair cut or her head shaved, she should wear a covering.
> —1 Corinthians 11:3-6

Headship is about submission. A woman's veil under the Old Testament (and in many contemporary cultures) indicated she was married and was under her husband's headship. Her veil was an outward display of an existing inner covenant. To remove that veil would dishonor her husband because its removal was a sign that she was available and not obligated to obey him.

Now let's look into the spiritual veil and its implications regarding legalism. The metaphorical head covering implies three realities we need to explore:

1. Blind submission as the focus
2. Critical thinking being suppressed
3. Ignorance being encouraged

Blind submission as the focus

Wearing a veil can indicate various levels of submission. Not all submission is the same, but wearing a veil is the outward declaration that you are submitted to headship of some type (i.e., a husband, God, or both). Your submission curtails your flexibility and freedom and plays a role in the choices you make.

For example, a veiled woman is not free to roam anywhere she pleases. Her head covering limits her movement and limits others from interacting with her for fear of disrespecting her husband or God. For this reason many legalistic believers have few friends, which limits their ability to have fun.

There is a parallel between the physical veil and the spiritual one. Physically, the veil presents the appearance of modesty; spiritually, it creates limitations. Preaching at a veil church (a church that requires their women to wear veils and their men to wear sackcloth) raises some sensitive issues. During my sermon in such a church, the Holy Spirit moved powerfully, and I ministered in the gifts of the Spirit. I approached a certain woman, and as I ministered to her, she spoke in tongues.

God was touching this woman, but another woman in the congregation ran up to pull the praying woman's veil over her head. Immediately, the praying woman stopped allowing God to touch her, and the Holy Spirit was quenched.

That moment left a deep impression on me. I realized the dear sister who ran up meant no harm. She was trying to keep her sister from violating Paul's warning against women prophesying without head coverings. She didn't realize the "help" she provided actually grieved the Holy Spirit.

This is an example of blind submission. Instead of thoroughly understanding a situation, you act in a ritualistic manner. Metaphorically, your understanding is limited by your veil. Your blind submission to the Scriptures or certain rules doesn't please God. But many legalistic believers are bound to what they know (or think they know). Submission has been continuously drilled into them until it's all they know, and it filters everything, including any preaching they hear.

Critical thinking being suppressed

The second implication regarding legalism is the suppression of critical thinking. During the lifetime of the apostle Paul a certain custom massively restricted critical thinking: Paul instructed women to remain silent in the church and not appear to usurp authority. This is a deep subject that we cannot adequately cover here, and whether Paul was simply respecting the customs of his day or dealing with his own legalism is a question for another time. But silence among the veiled women in the nascent church is pertinent to our study.

> Let your women keep silence in the churches: for it is not permitted unto them to speak; but they are commanded to be under obedience, as also saith the law. And if they will learn any thing, let them ask their husbands at home: for it is a shame for women to speak in the church.
> —1 Corinthians 14:34–35, kjv

The called-for silence is spiritually symbolic. Many believers attending legalistic churches are discouraged from engaging in critical thinking or even asking questions, with the latter being seen as dishonoring the pastor. In my past season in a legalistic denomination I remember sharing with my wife some concerns about the emphasis on submission and other doctrines. She would explain her perspective to me, but the infringement of critical thinking and the implied discomfort with questions troubled me. In such settings people end up obeying rules and other people without really knowing why!

Legalism discourages the asking of questions. Yet Scripture encourages us to be like the Bereans, who "were more open-minded than those in Thessalonica, and...listened eagerly to Paul's message....[and] searched the Scriptures day after day to see if Paul and Silas were teaching the truth" (Acts 17:11). The Bereans scrutinized every sermon they heard, yet they were considered *open-minded*!

My wife, who used to shush me when I asked questions, is now a Berean at heart, with active critical thinking skills and questions of her own. This is important for us all because asking questions provides access to information, encourages sound biblical decision-making, and honors both the Scriptures and the Holy Spirit.

Ignorance being encouraged

The final implication of legalism involves ignorance as the norm. If your whole Christian experience revolves around submission and not asking questions, you won't grow. Many believers within the legalistic culture are not studious about the Scriptures. In fact, the legalistic culture does not encourage Christians to pursue academics in the Word. In some denominations going to Bible school or seminary is equated with dishonoring the Holy Spirit!

Yet being ignorant of Bible truths produces anxiety. Believers in such settings are terrified (as I was) when they are called on to preach and teach. Why? Because outside of messages about the rules, nothing more can be said. The minds of legalistic believers are so veiled that they don't know what to say to God's people. So no matter what the sermon topic might be, the message will always focus on the rules.

Has revelation from Scripture been hitting you right in the face as you read this section? And is your soul struggling to embrace it? Remember you only know what you know, and what you have known makes no room for what you're hearing now. So rest easy, and let the Holy Spirit lead you.

VEIL OVER ISRAEL AND THE CURRENT CHURCH

What I'm about to share might be the most scale-removing, veil-lifting idea in this book. Let's start with a passage in Paul's words:

> We are not like Moses, who would put a veil over his face to prevent the Israelites from seeing the end of what was passing away. But their minds were made dull, for to this day the same veil remains when the old covenant is read. It has not been removed, because only in Christ is it taken away. Even to this day when Moses is read, a veil covers their hearts.
> —2 CORINTHIANS 3:13–15, NIV

Notice the first five words in the passage: "We are not like Moses." Let them sink deep into your heart and mind. The statement is almost monumental because 99 percent of legalistic believers, churches, and denominations are trying to be like Moses while preaching the gospel of Jesus Christ. *But we are not called to pattern ourselves after Moses or the Mosaic way of life.*

Paul helps us see the parallel between (1) how Moses covered his face with a veil (after having received the second set of tablets with the Ten Commandments and speaking to the children of Israel), and (2) how today's church uses veils. (See Exodus 34:33.) The children of Israel are a type of the church. Exodus 34:30 says they were afraid of Moses's radiant face when he descended from Mount Sinai. In Exodus 20:18, when Moses first received the Ten Commandments, the children of Israel put distance between themselves and Moses and begged for God not to speak to them directly. These texts show that the Israelites

» could not see the glory and

» were hardened in their minds.

The glory of God obscured

When your mind is veiled with religion but God manifests Himself anyway, seeing His glory is hard. As was true for Israel, the glory is often obscured today by the fire of God, which usually brings judgment. I believe this explains legalism's heavy emphasis on the fire of God instead of the glory of God. The glory is an unveiling of the person of God and the weightiness the revelation entails. The glory is not the same as the fire of God. Instead of personhood, the fire speaks of judgment. This is why the children of Israel couldn't handle the radiance on Moses's face. This is unfortunate because Moses is a type of Christ, who came to redeem us.

Moses didn't understand the lasting spiritual effect that covering his face for the people's sake would have on them. If you are a pastor, the church you shepherd will never grow beyond your level of understanding. Whatever you embrace or reject as truth from Scripture, the congregation will do likewise. Are you legalistic, judgmental, and harsh in expressing your faith? Then the people you pastor will follow your example. Do you shy away from intimacy with God or from seeing His glory? If so, the people in your church will do the same.

A hardened mind

When Moses veiled his face, the mindset of the children of Israel was darkened, or made ignorant. He put a physical veil on his face, but a spiritual veil was placed on their hearts. Moses played a part in first-century Israel's stiff-necked condition and inability to understand the gospel of God's grace. The minds of those who cannot accept God's grace are so hardened that nothing can penetrate them unless it conforms to what they already know.

Recently, I watched on social media as a Latino pastor preached the most legalistic message I have heard in quite some time. He made a blanket statement that any church leader who has joined a soccer team will go to hell, along with any women who are playing basketball. As I watched the pastor and his congregation, my heart broke. The people screamed, "Amen, Pastor!" as he spent more time insulting people than preaching the gospel.

For a church leader to insult people from the pulpit, and for the people in the pews to shout amen when he does, minds have to be hardened. Legalism is a false gospel and a doctrine of demons! Legalism is producing "the appearance of godliness, but denying its power" (2 Tim. 3:5, ESV).

While we're on the subject of the hardened mind, let me pose a revealing question and offer an answer. Q: Is grace a license to sin? A: Whenever churches gather and emphasize a Mosaic system of rules and regulations, minds are hardened more and more, and people become increasingly intolerant and mean-spirited. As a result, they have a very hard time embracing grace as anything other than a license to sin.

If you are a pastor or leader, I can tell you that sound scriptural preaching on the grace of God is not misinterpreted as a license to sin. God's grace causes believers to turn away from sin. The goodness of His grace does not tempt us toward licentiousness but empowers us to fall in love with Jesus, abide in Him, and bear much fruit. (See John 15:7–8.)

Breaking Free and Moving Forward

Removing the veil

What is the answer for removing the veil? A fresh revelation of Jesus! It is a matter of allowing Him to show you who He is. We saw in 2 Corinthians 3:14 how our minds are hardened. But verse 16 says, "Whenever someone turns to the Lord, the veil is taken away."

The only way to break the veil of religiosity and legalism is to allow Jesus to fully reveal Himself and remove the veil. Removing the veil in your own strength will prove futile. You must turn to the Lord and allow the Holy Spirit to do it. If you truly want to break free from a works-based gospel, then call on the Spirit of God now and ask Him to break any chains that have held you. Let the Spirit change everything in you that has leaned toward Moses, and He will lead you to become Christlike instead. The Holy Spirit will change your view of Scripture, your understanding of sanctification, and the way you see other believers.

> For the Lord is the Spirit, and wherever the Spirit of the Lord is, there is freedom. So all of us who have had that veil removed can see and reflect the glory of the Lord. And the Lord—who is the Spirit—makes us more and more like him as we are changed into his glorious image.
> —2 Corinthians 3:17–18

After the veil is removed

The writer of Hebrews describes three things that happen after the Holy Spirit removes the veil:

> By his death, Jesus opened a *new* and *life-giving* way through the curtain into the Most Holy Place. And since we have a great High Priest who rules over God's house, *let us go right into the presence of God* with sincere hearts fully trusting him. For our guilty consciences have been sprinkled with Christ's

blood to make us clean, and our bodies have been washed with pure water.
—Hebrews 10:20–22, emphasis added

A new way

The first change is that you break away from monotonous and stagnating service to God. In its place comes a fresh way of serving that was previously hidden by the veil of religion. Legalism thrives on routine. But the Holy Spirit will show you a new way to honor God, read Scripture, pray, worship Him, and fellowship with your church family. Let the Lord reveal what *new* will look like.

A life-giving way

Your service and worship to God will be not only fresh and new but vital and life-giving. This is the resurrection, which causes dead things to come alive. Your prayer life, Bible-study time, and relationship with the Lord will be revitalized. Spending time with Jesus will be not an obligation but a joyous time of relationship with Jesus that overflows to others.

Most unbelievers aren't attracted to the Jesus that legalistic believers serve. John 10:10 says the real Jesus came to give us abundant life. The most life-giving Christians are the ones who first receive abundant life. And they are the people who win the most souls. There is nothing dull about life in Christ!

Direct access to God's presence

Legalism causes believers to run away from God, but grace causes us to approach Him and run to Him! Hebrews 10:22 urges us to enter God's presence with assurance. I remember when this was hard for me to do because I was taught God was so holy, and I was such a sinner. So I assumed I could never measure up. But Jesus measured up on my behalf, and I now know that access is my portion.

You might be wondering, "What about my daily sins?" Well, remember: "Our guilty consciences have been sprinkled with Christ's blood to make us clean, and our bodies have been washed with pure water" (Heb. 10:22). Jesus' atoning sacrifice paid the penalty for your sin and gave you continuous access to the Father, so you can lift your hands in worship without feeling condemned. Confess your daily sins before the Lord and remain in His presence! And pray this prayer:

> *Lord, thank You for continuing to remove the veil so I can freely breathe in Your Spirit and clearly hear and understand what You are saying. Lord, please continue flushing out any remnants of legalism from my system! And as I read Your Word, let it be the antidote to any religiosity that still occupies my mind and heart. In Jesus' name, I pray. Amen.*

Chapter 9

MANIPULATING WITH GUILT AND SHAME

Don't let anyone condemn you for what you eat or drink, or for not celebrating certain holy days or new moon ceremonies or Sabbaths. For these rules are only shadows of the reality yet to come. And Christ himself is that reality.
—COLOSSIANS 2:16–17

WHEN GUILT AND shame are manipulated, religion (including Christianity) becomes toxic. So I am emphatically calling for reformation—not just change and not revolution but reformation. Our Lord Jesus dealt with toxic religion head-on. So did the early church and the apostle Paul, who spoke bluntly about legalism, writing, "I wish that those who are troubling you [by teaching that circumcision is necessary for salvation] would even [go all the way and] castrate themselves!" (Gal. 5:12, AMP).

Paul was not passive about this issue. To break free from legalism's grip, we must share his mentality. After conducting hundreds of deliverance sessions, I can say the hardest demon to cast out is the religious spirit! Legalism, tradition, and self-righteousness are stubborn, and we must contend against them with determination.

Why is reformation necessary? Because mere change can be undone by one zealot who stirs the pot and draws a crowd. This happened repeatedly in ancient Israel and Judah. All it took was one evil king to reverse every good work of the good king who preceded him. This is why I am not a big fan of change, which can take years and drain all your energy and resources. When I first pastored a denominational church, I had to get permission from the elders to make a change, devote Bible studies to the reasons for the change, discuss it at a board meeting, and hold a corporate meeting for a vote. By the time everything was done, we were drained, and so was our passion for the change.

The slow version of change I just described is not viable. However, I absolutely do not advocate for a revolution or revolt of any kind. Revolutions bring change through destruction, and even Jesus did not set out to destroy the law. (See Matthew 5:17.) Jesus was not a revolutionary. Therefore, I'm not looking to ignite a revolution.

Let's be honest. Many of us started the journey of faith in legalism. God allowed us to begin there. And to some degree we have what we have as a result. We don't need to destroy a system that helped us back then. Nor should we weaponize any revelations about freedom and force them on our local churches. We're not called to belittle pastors and leaders in the name of reformation.

I see reformation as an upgrade to a previous system that needs improvement. Reformation always honors the system and the people within it. I honor my legalistic brothers and sisters in Christ, and I love them dearly. (I used to be one of them!) And I love the hyperconservative churches that helped start me in ministry; I am a byproduct of legalism, a son of the legalistic Pentecostal churches. I believe God has sent me to pour back into that movement. Nowhere in this book did I attempt to dishonor anyone. Jesus did not dishonor the Law of Moses. He often referred to the law and then shared an even higher standard with the words "but I say unto you" (in Matthew 5:22, 28, and 32, KJV, for example). The Lord Jesus loved God's people then, and He loves them now. He will never dishonor His church, but He will correct it.

Reformation is essential because something that is reformed can never return to what it used to be. What existed before the reformation no longer exists in the way it once did. The differences reformation makes are permanent. Paul never dishonored the Old Covenant but addressed the permanent change the New Covenant achieved, saying, "If the old way, which has been replaced, was glorious, how much more glorious is the new, which remains forever!" (2 Cor. 3:11).

I believe that after reading this book, your mindset will have shifted. That is true reformation—an authorized system upgrade. In this chapter we'll view that upgrade in relation to several minor issues that still plague the church. As you consider them, remember they are perpetuated through manipulation, which is not always malicious but is always harmful.

MANIPULATED

When Jesus ministered in Israel, four hundred years of prophetic silence caused the people to value rabbinic and Pharisaic opinion in the extreme. The last prophet who spoke before this period was Malachi, who said a messenger was coming to prepare the way of the promised Messiah. The prophetic silence that followed created a vacuum that was filled by interpreters of the law. I believe that at this point, the traditions of men began to replace the Scriptures.

This imbalance of spiritual influence was unhealthy, and it is similar to the kind of imbalances I've described in today's system of legalism. Although the intent might not be malicious, the resulting manipulation corrupts what is godly. This process starts in the mind when one person influences another via suggestion and teaching, shaping their worldview and causing behavior modification.

Paul warned against this. Speaking about unity and maturity within the body of Christ, he urged "that we henceforth be no more children, tossed to and fro, and carried about with every wind of doctrine, by *the sleight of men*, and cunning craftiness, whereby they lie in wait to deceive" (Eph. 4:14, KJV, emphasis added). What the apostle called "the sleight of men" is a kind of manipulation that can be perpetrated on us when we are immature in the Scriptures and easily moved by any wind of doctrine.

Studying God's Word anchors you in the bedrock of Scripture so you can easily detect and dispel falsehood. Otherwise, any charlatan can present a Bible verse or two and convince you they mean something other than God's full intent. Paul saw manipulation as evil, but it's also convenient. All a teacher needs are a pulpit and a congregation not grounded in orthodox Christianity. That is how man-made rules and traditions gain (false) preeminence over Christ.

Whether the intent of an influencer is innocent or not, an immature church is fertile ground for theological manipulation.

FEASTS AND OTHER JUDAIC MARKERS

A little ignorance goes a long way where misunderstanding and manipulation are concerned. One person with an interesting idea or "revelation" can lead many into confusion. A common example involves the keeping of the Sabbath days and Jewish festivals. Both get their share of attention in some Christian movements.

So should Gentile believers in Christ keep the Jewish festivals? The simple answer is Gentiles are not required to observe them. I am not sure why many who aren't of Jewish heritage choose to keep the ancient festivals. The Lord's brother, the apostle James, told the convened Jerusalem Council that only limited Jewish rules should be imposed:

> We should not make it difficult for the Gentiles who are turning to God. Instead, we should write and tell them to abstain from eating food offered to idols, from sexual immorality, from eating the meat of strangled animals, and from consuming blood. For these laws of Moses have been preached

in Jewish synagogues in every city on every Sabbath for many generations.

—Acts 15:19–21

This directive is clear and was documented in a letter, which the council circulated in the early church. When it was read in Antioch, "there was great joy throughout the church that day as [the messengers] read this encouraging message" (Acts 15:31).

When believers are forced to observe Jewish markers, the act of worshipping God externally rather than internally becomes burdensome. They develop intimacy with rituals but lose the essence of the divine intent, moving their hearts away from the preeminence of Christ. Without realizing it they grieve the Holy Spirit by trying to connect to God through an ordinance God is no longer blessing.

Although we respect their origins, we do not need to physically keep the Jewish festivals. Instead, we are keeping them through Christ. I confess that I read Acts 15:19–21 many, many times before I got it. Whether I never saw it or ignored it, I can't say. Either way, I was effectively blinded to the truth.

Pentecostalism or Pietism?

Before I write another word, let me say that singling out the Pentecostal movement is not my intent. I come from Pentecostalism and continue in the Pentecostal experience of speaking in other tongues. My roots in Pentecostalism run deep, and I was rising through the Latino Pentecostal ranks when my understanding of the Scriptures found conflict—not in the fundamental doctrine but in the extreme dogmas within my denomination.

What I noticed was a thin line separating true Pentecostalism (which begins with the Acts 2 account of the day of Pentecost) and what we would call pietism, which I briefly described in the introduction as an "emphasis on devotional experience and practices; affectation of devotion."[1] A pietistic movement began as a reform movement in the seventeenth century,[2] and it remains as "a recurring tendency within Christian history to emphasize Christian practice over theology and church order."[3]

Pietism requires a heavy emphasis on how much you are willing to sacrifice or surrender to God to solidify your salvation or to be "on fire" for Him. There is a constant requirement of "going all out for God." Pious as that sounds, it leads believers into guilt because no human being is capable of sacrificing everything. We are works in progress, and the Holy Spirit is helping us crucify our flesh. There is nothing wrong with being on fire for God, but Scripture doesn't tell us to be on fire for Him. However, Matthew 16:24 does tell us to deny ourselves, take up our crosses, and follow Christ. And Galatians 5:24 calls us to crucify our flesh.

Because I could never "surrender enough," I was riddled with guilt and filled with torment. Because my nine-to-five job kept me from praying in tongues for three hours a day, my pietism wracked my soul and probably the souls of others in our church. Sermon after sermon reminded me to surrender everything to Jesus. So week after week, I tried surrendering enough. Eventually, I became exhausted, embittered, and worried about whether such surrender was even biblical.

Then one day I read this verse: "By that one offering he [Jesus] forever made perfect those who are being made holy" (Heb. 10:14). Those words changed everything for me; an overwhelming peace gripped my soul, and I finally entered the "Sabbath rest" mentioned in Hebrews 4:9 (ESV). Yes, we should surrender all we are to the call of God. But we also need to enter into true biblical rest. When I did, my prayer life and my surrender to Jesus hit another level, I sought God more fervently than ever, and I have continued to do so.

TRUE WORSHIP AND WALKING IN LOVE

I never want to (1) worship God through a ritual He no longer endorses, or (2) ritualize an ordinance and become dogmatic about it. Isaiah warned against replacing true worship with a well-polished exterior:

> You hypocrites! Isaiah was right when he prophesied about you, for he wrote, "These people honor me with their lips, but their hearts are far from me. Their worship is a farce, for they teach man-made ideas as commands from God."
>
> —MATTHEW 15:7–9

Anything done outside its season is idolatry. Certain laws God established in the Old Testament served as types and shadows of Christ. Keeping the Sabbath on a certain day is one. The question of whether the Sabbath should be on Saturday or Sunday would require a book of its own. There are countless books that address the larger doctrinal issues such as the Sabbath, women preachers, and divorce. My focus is on dogmatic bylaws, man-made traditions, and the question "Is it lawful?" Therefore, I want to look into Sabbath keeping—not so much about the day of the week but about what God allows on such days.

So what is lawful on the Sabbath? Is God annoyed because much of the church gathers on Sunday for worship and the Lord's Supper? Is that lawful? We know the Sabbath involves rest. We also know that in Christ we rest from the former labor of justifying ourselves through our works. Instead, we rest and trust in the finished work of the cross. So when is the true Sabbath, and what work is lawful for us to do?

I believe Jesus answered these questions when He said the following:

> Now I am giving you a new commandment: Love each other. Just as I have loved you, you should love each other. Your love for one another will prove to the world that you are my disciples.
>
> —JOHN 13:34–35

Paul also expressed this idea in his letter to the Romans:

> Owe nothing to anyone except for your obligation to love one another. If you love your neighbor, you will fulfill the requirements of God's law. For the commandments say, "You must not commit adultery. You must not murder. You must not steal. You must not covet." These—and other such commandments—are summed up in this one commandment: "Love your neighbor as yourself."
> —ROMANS 13:8–9

Walking in love sums up all the commandments, including those about the Sabbath, baptism, and the like.

Scripture provides two strong examples of breaking the law while walking in love. One is from the Old Testament and one from the New:

- » When King Saul had David on the run, David asked Ahimelech the priest for bread to feed his men. The only bread available was "the Bread of the Presence that was placed before the LORD in the Tabernacle. It had just been replaced that day with fresh bread" (1 Sam. 21:6). David gave the bread to his men because they were hungry.

- » On a particular Sabbath, as Jesus and His hungry disciples walked through the fields, the disciples "began breaking off some heads of grain and eating them" (Matt. 12:1). "When the Pharisees saw it, they said to [Jesus], 'Look, your disciples are doing what is not lawful to do on the Sabbath.' He said to them, 'Have you not read what David did when he was hungry, and those who were with him: how he entered the house of God and ate the bread of the Presence, which it was not lawful for him to eat nor for those who were with him, but only for the priests?'" (Matt. 12:2–4, ESV). Jesus allowed His disciples to eat because they were hungry.

Legalistic believers tend to keep the law so strictly that allowing their men to go hungry could seem wise. They misunderstand the law's original intent and get trapped by the letter of it. I understand their predicament; back in the day, I probably would have starved myself and my men. Thank God for grace! I now see that God put me in scenarios where I was required to walk in love and break the letter of the law. He was trying to break my legalism!

Has God put you in such situations? Might He be orchestrating them so you can see His heart? Is He challenging your understanding of the Scriptures in order to deliver you from man-made rules that forbid you to walk in love? If you sense your mindset is shifting, the fear of slipping into rebellion might still keep you sitting on the fence. Don't worry! You love God too much to rebel. Allow Him to guide you into His mindset. Your dilemma has everything to do with being born on a Friday.

Born on a Friday

Let me explain: Being born on a Friday is a metaphor I have taught for more than a decade. It's about people whose very birth causes the system to break its own rules! Let's start unpacking this idea with a verse from John's Gospel:

> If a man on the sabbath day receive circumcision, that the law of Moses should not be broken; are ye angry at me, because I have made a man every whit whole on the sabbath day?
> —John 7:23, KJV

The context of this verse is controversy: People were challenging Jesus for healing a man on the Sabbath. Jesus reminded them that all newborn boys were commanded to be circumcised on the eighth day. However, some of them would be born on Fridays, so the eighth day would fall on the Sabbath. Technically, the priests performing circumcisions on Sabbath days were breaking the law. But unless they did, those children would be cut off forever from their people.

Neither the priests nor the babies had any say about when the boys would be born. The priests' only reasonable choice was to make an accommodation: The status quo had to be disrupted for the babies' sakes!

Were you born on a (metaphorical) Friday? Does everything within you scream for freedom and challenge the status quo? Maybe you disrupt things wherever you are, and every time you join a church, they break the rules so you can serve in their house. Something about you makes other people break their norms and be free.

If that describes you, church leaders have noticed, and some may have called you a rebel. The fact is, you didn't choose to be born on a Friday, and they don't know how to handle you. You might even wonder whether something is wrong with you. You seem so outspoken about the things of God that you wonder why you can't just be a good Christian and submit to legalism like other people do.

But you can't! We all were born on a Friday, and the church has broken its own rules to graft us in. I had no choice but to realize that God's hand was on me. When I was imprisoned in the early 1990s, there was no available baptism tank, so I could not fulfill the command to be baptized until after my release. And yet God has kept me. Wherever I went in the body of Christ, I was placed in leadership. When I first came home from jail and joined my family's church, the pastor and leaders saw the calling on my life and immediately asked me to preach on a Sunday. I wasn't a church member, and I had not yet been baptized in water—two strict requirements for preaching from that pulpit! The elders bypassed the rules because they believed I had a message from the Lord.

There are so many other questions on my mind, but for now I would just urge us not to major on minors, a practice that leads only to cultural elitism. Just know that God is raising a group of people to be reformers in our day, and ask yourself, "Am I one?"

DOCTRINAL ELITISM

From the days of the apostle Paul, doctrinal elitism has reared its head. This was the main issue in the church at Corinth, where many claimed to follow this or that church leader's "philosophy" over the others. We still see many Christian persuasions, with people choosing to follow one over the other. Over the centuries, the names of groups might have changed, but the elitism remains. Paul came down hard on it because it is divisive.

> I appeal to you, brothers, by the name of our Lord Jesus Christ, that all of you agree, and that there be no divisions among you, but that you be united in the same mind and the same judgment. For it has been reported to me by Chloe's people that there is quarreling among you, my brothers. What I mean is that each one of you says, "I follow Paul," or "I follow Apollos," or "I follow Cephas," or "I follow Christ." Is Christ divided? Was Paul crucified for you? Or were you baptized in the name of Paul?
>
> —1 CORINTHIANS 1:10–13, ESV

Anybody can fall into this trap. Nobody's theology is perfect, not even mine. Each of us needs to study for ourselves and allow the Holy Spirit to show us what He wants us to see. Sometimes what He reveals complements the messages of our favorite Christian teachers, authors, pastors, and leaders. But sometimes it raises questions. Ultimately, we have to let go of our notions and elitism and embrace what the Spirit reveals.

Elitism has many different looks, but one marker is a sense of superiority or even strict separatism. In some churches and denominations the rules established by the elders become law, and everything—one's dating choices, for example—must be sanctioned by the elders. There are too many complex rules to mention here, but anyone in the congregation who breaks one could be shunned and excommunicated.

In chapter 6 we talked about the seat of Moses as a place of authority. The control of doctrine in twenty-first-century churches and denominations reminds me of what Jesus said about that:

> The teachers of religious law and the Pharisees are the official interpreters of the law of Moses. So practice and obey whatever they tell you, but don't follow their example. For they don't practice what they teach. They crush people with unbearable religious demands and never lift a finger to ease the burden. "Everything they do is for show."
> —MATTHEW 23:2–5

When any human being is given authority, there is a mixing of human nature and God's absolute truth. Therefore, religious elites tend to devise man-made traditions that collide with Scripture in some way. Consider the example of *rumspringa*—a practice among some Amish groups that allows teens at sixteen "to explore otherwise forbidden or strictly regulated behaviours before making the choice to commit to the church."[4] Some of these youths have sex before deciding whether they will join the church for life.

Did the Holy Spirit initiate rumspringa? I don't think so. Rumspringa is a man-made tradition—one of many in hyperconservative circles. Whether the rules involve electricity, separatism, superstitions and practices for warding off evil spirits, or esoteric ideas about cars with black-painted bumpers, only truly scriptural principles will last.

My point is not to criticize denominations that have become immersed in questionable ideas; I am merely stating the facts, as my brothers in these denominations have explained them to me. They know I am being truthful, and I know they are saved people. They love God and love their churches. Even so, some are praying for God to bring freedom and return the movement to what His Spirit reveals.

I believe a great Spirit-led revival is coming to these churches, and you will see it with your own eyes!

Form of Godliness

When you are trapped in doctrinal elitism, you end up having a "form of godliness" but denying its power (2 Tim. 3:5, KJV). The New Living Translation says, "They will act religious, but they will reject the power that could make them godly. Stay away from people like that!" (2 Tim. 3:5).

Elitism causes you to proselytize your views of doctrine when you're called to preach the doctrine of Christ. The power of God can be manifested only through preaching Christ crucified! Many people think I'm running around the world preaching the "gospel of deliverance" and nothing else. That is not the case, but I get their point. It's easy to get trapped in a certain kind of gospel—of holiness, healing, financial breakthrough, or signs and wonders, for example. But that becomes formulaic, and formulas have no power. Paul understood that limited views of the kingdom produce a powerless Christianity. Instead, the sum of everything we preach needs to involve Christ's death, burial, and resurrection—that's it! Side doctrines add no value.

The law has shortcomings in relation to the message of Christ crucified. The writer of the Book of Hebrews understood this and explained that the law revealed how the entrance to fellowship with God was blocked.

> By these regulations the Holy Spirit revealed that the entrance to the Most Holy Place was not freely open as long as the Tabernacle and the system it represented were still in use. This is an illustration pointing to the present time. For the gifts and sacrifices that the priests offer is not able to cleanse the consciences of the people who bring them. For that old

> system deals only with food and drink and various cleansing ceremonies—physical regulations that were in effect only until a better system could be established.
> —HEBREWS 9:8–10

When someone who has converted to Christ tries to observe the ceremonial, festival aspects of the Old Testament, they effectively reblock the entrance the blood of Jesus made possible. The Old Testament style of worship is an inferior system compared with the better covenant that Christ made possible.

This might sting, but it needs to be said: The legalistic, religious system of worship is inferior. Grace is superior and is glorious. "If the old way, which brings condemnation, was glorious, how much more glorious is the new way, which makes us right with God!" (2 Cor. 3:9).

The only way you can resist the covenant described in this book is to embrace a Moses style of worship. But Paul said, "*We are not like Moses*, who put a veil over his face so the people of Israel would not see the glory, even though it was destined to fade away" (2 Cor. 3:13, emphasis added).

We are not like Moses! Anything not centered on Jesus and the gospel of grace is like Moses! Moses was God's chosen leader for his time, and he pointed to Christ. However, when Christ came, God's grace came and detached those who believe in Christ from the ceremonialism and observance of days, feasts, new moons, and other rituals. The gospel of grace is built on a better system. Holiness might sound the best, but it isn't. Holiness is important, but it points to grace. (See 2 Corinthians 1:12.)

BREAKING FREE AND MOVING FORWARD

Complete in Him

Understanding will help you live the gospel of grace. First, know that you are complete in Christ. Rest in His work of salvation, and you will see you don't need to add anything or take anything away. Your sufficiency is in Christ alone.

> Ye are complete in him, which is the head of all principality and power: in whom also ye are circumcised with the circumcision made without hands, in putting off the body of the sins of the flesh by the circumcision of Christ: buried with him in baptism, wherein also ye are risen with him through the faith of the operation of God, who hath raised him from the dead.
> —Colossians 2:10–12, kjv

When you know you are complete in Christ, you feel no need to "circumcise" yourself because Christ has circumcised your heart. You don't need to do anything or add any rules of holiness. Just rest in Christ, who is complete. If the devil comes knocking, let Christ be your answer. He is ruling over every principality and power.

No condemnation

Second, please understand that well-meaning, sincere, but legalistic believers might criticize or even condemn your nonobservance of certain regulations. Don't let them interrupt your move toward freedom. The apostle Paul said, "Don't let anyone condemn you.... For these rules are only shadows of the reality yet to come. And Christ himself is that reality" (Col. 2:16–17).

Just be bold and stand your ground. Refuse to be shamed by those who misunderstand and even fight against you. Remember that the preconversion Saul of Tarsus fought Christ's followers, yet God used him mightily. So pray for people who oppose you. Don't allow your heart to grow bitter, but don't budge either. Just keep your eyes on Jesus.

Personal persuasion

Third, be patient with those who still favor strict rules. Remember that legalism is not a topic worthy of creating division with our Christian brothers and sisters. You might long to shake the religiosity out of them, but give them a chance to embrace a new mindset. And know this: Many people will never change. Still, you need to respect and not judge them. Take some tips from Paul:

> Accept other believers who are weak in faith, and don't argue with them about what they think is right or wrong....One person believes it's all right to eat anything. But another...will eat only vegetables....In the same way, some think one day is more holy than another day, while others think every day is alike. You should each be fully convinced that whichever day you choose is acceptable. Those who worship the Lord on a special day do it to honor him. Those who eat any kind of food do so to honor the Lord, since they give thanks to God before eating. And those who refuse to eat certain foods also want to please the Lord and give thanks to God....Whether we live or die, we belong to the Lord. Christ died and rose again for this very purpose—to be Lord both of the living and of the dead. So why do you condemn another believer? Why do you look down on another believer? Remember, we will all stand before the judgment seat of God.
> —ROMANS 14:1–2, 5–6, 8–10

After I spent many years trying to force people to change their views, the passage above set me free. I hope it sets you free too! Just respect others, and allow them to follow their own consciences as they try to honor God. If you're walking in grace, don't look down on those trapped in legalism. Whatever camp you're in, stop condemning the other camps. Romans 14:3 says, "God has accepted them"!

Living free

Finally, Paul encouraged the Galatian church to live freely, as he did. (See Galatians 4:12, below.) That's a heavy statement coming from a man once steeped in legalism. He wanted everyone to know that if he could live free, they could too. Because some believers in Christ were turning back to the law, he gave them a reminder:

> So now that you know God (or should I say, now that God knows you), why do you want to go back again and become slaves once more to the weak and useless spiritual principles of this world? You are trying to earn favor with God by observing certain days or months or seasons or years. I fear for you. Perhaps all my hard work with you was for nothing. Dear brothers and sisters, I plead with you to live as I do in freedom from these things, for I have become like you Gentiles—free from those laws.
>
> —GALATIANS 4:9–12

When Paul mentioned the weak things that enslaved people, he was not talking about sin but about returning to a religious mindset. In other words, whatever you do and no matter how hard it gets, do not revert to legalism! I know how tough that is when condemnation and criticism are all you know. It was hard for me. Plus, I worried I would end up abusing grace and using it as a license to sin. Well, that hasn't happened yet. The Holy Spirit helped me, like He helped Paul and will help you! Don't feel guilty about walking in freedom! That is your inheritance in Christ!

Lord, I ask that You continually lead me toward freedom. Help me distinguish fair criticism from legalistic forms of judgment that are meant to interrupt my advance toward freedom. Help me not be judgmental toward those who don't yet realize or are not yet ready to acknowledge legalism's hold on them. Help me bless others and not burden them as You lead them by Your Spirit, according to the timing You know is best. I ask these things in Jesus' name! Amen.

Chapter 10

IDOLIZING OLD TESTAMENT PARADIGMS

The old system under the law of Moses was only a shadow, a dim preview of the good things to come, not the good things themselves.
—Hebrews 10:1

APPEARANCE MATTERS. DESPITE my youthful belief that nobody cared what I was wearing, my mom taught me my choices spoke loudly. Now my wife reminds me to consider the statement my appearance is making. She's talking not about petty rules but about whether my attire is in sync with my person. Scripture says that out "of the abundance of the heart" the mouth speaks (Luke 6:45, KJV). But everything about us speaks—even our appearance.

This truth doesn't only apply to people. The appearance of your church building speaks of the body's worldview. That is why some churches resemble the tabernacle of Moses, while some look like social clubs, and some emulate synagogues. The church my wife and I came from evoked a living room vibe, with actual sofas on the platform. Some African American churches reserve one very large, ornate chair on the platform for the senior pastor's use. Whatever the style, a church building represents the biblical and personal views of the leadership and congregation.

Whether it's your personal wardrobe or the structure in which you gather for corporate worship, there is a desire to look a certain way. For example, your appearance reflects you. But you also mirror the people and philosophies you favor. Of course, your mirroring is based on your interpretation of who and what you favor, and that's where things get confusing.

Do you remember when Jesus shocked the Jews by speaking about their temple? He said, "Do you see all these buildings? I tell you the truth, they will be completely demolished. Not one stone will be left on top of another!" (Matt. 24:2). The people likely mistook Jesus' words for malice, but He was not malicious. He was prophesying truthfully, and those who were offended missed the types and shadows that were in play. They were offended not only by Jesus' words but by Jesus Himself.

We need to carefully discern the views we express and the preferences that drive our views. It is vitally important that we honor God's original intent and not worship a copy. We need clarity about the essence of what God has said. And we need to understand why He inspired what was written. These are the things that should govern our most internal beliefs. Then we will discern which commandments and prescriptions in the Old and New Testaments are to be followed literally, and which are to be honored by way of remembrance.

We can explore this idea by studying the things God's people have rightly or wrongly venerated over the millennia.

BY WAY OF REMEMBRANCE ONLY

The Lord's Communion is the perfect place to begin. Partaking of this sacrament is *not* a sign of legalism. We are commanded by Jesus to partake frequently when we gather. "On the first day of the week" the early church shared in the Lord's Supper as they "gathered with the local believers" (Acts 20:7). But when Jesus gave the first command in this regard, "he took some bread and gave thanks to God for it. Then he broke it in pieces and gave it to the disciples, saying, 'This is my body, which is given for you. Do this in remembrance of me'" (Luke 22:19).

Jesus described this as an act of remembrance rather than veneration. He rarely told His followers to continue a practice after His departure. He did call us to continue in Holy Communion, but not by way of idolatry. That means we don't worship the act; we worship Him who showed us the act. We revere its significance when we gather with the saints, but we don't worship the copy. By that I mean we don't make rules that require a certain Communion frequency denoting holiness or determining whether we are saved. Nor should we go rule crazy by trying to replicate the original elements of unleavened bread and wine. We don't worship bread and wine; we reverence these elements because of what they represent: the body and blood of Jesus.

There is no end to the legalism that can ensue when you worship the copy. Some churches prohibit the taking of Holy Communion by those who fail to follow a church bylaw, are not church members, or are struggling with a certain sin. I have seen many believers remain in the pews while the rest of the congregation approaches the Communion table. You can imagine the rejection experienced by those who were considered "unworthy"!

The question is whether such restrictions honor the essence of the Lord's Communion. Wasn't His body broken for those who considered themselves unworthy? Wasn't His blood shed for those who struggled with sin? The Lord's table is a liberating act, not a legalistic command. Jesus allowed even Judas to partake of the bread and wine. Should we prevent people who desperately need God's mercy and forgiveness from partaking of the Lord's table?

I am not speaking here about those who mock the Lord's table. They need to be rebuked. In 1 Corinthians 11:17–34 the apostle Paul corrected the Corinthian church for its excesses and lack of reverence for the Communion. But reducing the Lord's table to a mere ritual and then idolizing the ritual is also out of order.

Bear in mind that many issues like this one revolve around the tendency to venerate a copy, in this case the remembrance we know as Holy Communion. What we are meant to pursue is intimacy with the reality behind the copy. This is an age-old tendency, and the writer of the Book of Hebrews addressed it. The following verse reminded the Hebrew Christians that many acts of service and worship to YHWH were copies of something yet to come.

> They serve in a system of worship that is only a copy, a shadow of the real one in heaven. For when Moses was getting ready to build the Tabernacle, God gave him this warning: "Be sure that you make everything according to the pattern I have shown you here on the mountain."
>
> —Hebrews 8:5

Many of us fail by not promptly and lovingly correcting the Old Testament ritualism that entangles our brethren. By remaining silent, we seem to say that the ritualism is harmless or even beneficial to our worship of Jesus. As a result, it takes root, becomes dogma, leads to a commandment, and eventually justifies condemning those who don't obey our rule. This can happen with Holy Communion but also with circumcision.

The Copy of Circumcision

I have concluded that in Paul's day, the movement he most opposed was the circumcision—again, Jewish believers who converted to Christianity but believed you had to obey Old Covenant circumcision in order to be saved. Paul and Barnabas fiercely and publicly refuted this movement. While they ministered in Antioch, "some men from Judea arrived and began to teach the believers: 'Unless you are circumcised as required by the law of Moses, you cannot be saved'" (Acts 15:1).

Paul and Barnabas "disagreed" and argued "vehemently" against this teaching (Acts 15:2). Eventually, the church called

Paul, Barnabas, and others to Jerusalem to discuss the matter with church leaders there.

Those of the circumcision aggressively proselytized in Antioch and gained a huge following. In chapter 9 we saw how the Jerusalem Council addressed legalism within the fledgling church. Following their deliberations, they sent Paul and Barnabas back to Antioch with a letter clarifying what was and was not required of new converts. They determined that Jewish festivals and circumcision were not required. They did, however, counsel believers to "abstain from eating food offered to idols, from consuming blood or the meat of strangled animals, and from sexual immorality" (Acts 15:29).

The council's decision regarding circumcision lifted a burden, especially from older men who had been told they must cut their foreskin. This rule gained traction among Christians when they misunderstood God's intent, copied a commandment that had already been fulfilled, and venerated it. Originally, circumcision was instituted as a sign of the circumcised heart that would become possible in Christ. Colossians 2:11 then explained circumcision in light of the cross, saying, "When you came to Christ, you were 'circumcised,' but not by a physical procedure. Christ performed a spiritual circumcision—the cutting away of your sinful nature." Once Jesus completed His work of salvation, the cutting of a man's flesh was no longer necessary!

When the divine intent is lost in translation, we act on what we think is true. Many sincere pastors and leaders who try to copy the instruction of Old Testament passages end up drifting toward extremism. Many years ago, I visited the church of an administrative bishop in the denomination. I saw in front of the pulpit some steam and twelve rocks that the bishop had used to illustrate a message from Joshua 4. The service had apparently been very anointed, and the bishop left the twelve rocks on the platform.

During my visit, I preached from the same pulpit. Afterward, I touched the rocks and learned only authorized people were allowed to touch them. Remember that the rocks were only a copy, a remembrance of a biblical event, yet they were being venerated and treated as holy articles. In all fairness, this can happen to anybody over anything in Scripture, provided clarity is lacking or the scriptural intent is misinterpreted.

THE COPY OF THE OLD SYSTEM

I have witnessed or been part of many stories like the one I just shared. I'm not trying to heap criticism on the legalistic churches that taught me many wonderful things. It is fair to say, however, that I learned some things from those churches, and I'm still detoxing from them. So instead of throwing stones, I'm still learning about the stones I once threw at people who disagreed with legalism. Sadly, I realize what the writer of Hebrews understood:

> The old system under the law of Moses was only a shadow, a dim preview of the good things to come, not the good things themselves. The sacrifices under that system were repeated again and again, year after year, but they were never able to provide perfect cleansing for those who came to worship.
> —HEBREWS 10:1

Distinguishing between shadow and reality is imperative. "A shadow is a dark area on a surface where light from a light source is blocked by an object."[1] The object is three-dimensional, but the shadow's image is two-dimensional. To see the Scriptures in shadow form is to miss the third dimension that makes them a reality and not a ritual.

Christ is the reality; He sums up all types, shadows, copies, parallels, enigmas, systems, and symbols. Christ is all and fills all! (See Ephesians 1:23.) Some churches have replicas of the ark of the covenant, table of showbread, or table of incense. There is nothing wrong with these decorative items, but venerating them is legalistic. Especially where replicas of the ark of the covenant are concerned, I take issue with attempts to invoke the tabernacle of Moses. Why?

Because "these rules are only shadows of the reality yet to come. And Christ himself is that reality" (Col. 2:17).

Personally, I don't want a Mosaic or Davidic experience in church. I want to focus on Jesus, who is the object of my worship. Instead of the shekinah that touched the Levites, I desire the touch of Jesus. I don't want the cloud; I want the Son who will return in the clouds!

THE COPY OF THE BRONZE SNAKE

We talked earlier about the bronze serpent God commanded Moses to make in the wilderness. Because the people later worshipped it, Hezekiah destroyed it. To this day, it is a stumbling block to some Christians breaking out of legalism.

In Numbers 21:8-9 we see that God used the bronze serpent in healing Israelites who'd been bitten by snakes. They were poisoned by actual snakes and healed through the use of a replica snake. Both of these were real events.

It might seem that the story ended there, but it didn't. When Jesus was talking with Nicodemus, He told him that hidden in the story of the bronze serpent was the future work He was to accomplish by being lifted up on a cross and dying for the sins of the world (John 3:14). But Nicodemus did not understand that. Why? He was seeing only a copy and shadow in two dimensions.

Jesus told Nicodemus he needed to be born again, and Nicodemus asked, "How are these things possible?" (John 3:9). "Jesus replied, 'You are a respected Jewish teacher, and yet you don't understand these things?'" (v. 10).

> "How are these things possible?" Nicodemus asked. Jesus replied, "You are a respected Jewish teacher, and yet you don't understand these things? I assure you, we tell you what we know and have seen, and yet you won't believe our testimony. But if you don't believe me when I tell you about earthly things, how can you possibly believe if I tell you about heavenly

> things? No one has ever gone to heaven and returned. But the
> Son of Man has come down from heaven."
> —John 3:9–13

This is what happens when legalism dominates the mind of the believer. We can misunderstand matters because we miss their essence or significance. The religious person may read the story of Moses and the bronze serpent and make a doctrine out of it that leads to idolatry and possibly even to worshipping the snake. This is what happened to the children of Israel. They began to worship the bronze serpent and even gave it a name. This is the reason Hezekiah acted in 2 Kings 18:4 to remove pagan shrines, break up the bronze serpent, and destroy other religious articles.

> He removed the pagan shrines, smashed the sacred pillars, and cut down the Asherah poles. He broke up the bronze serpent that Moses had made, because the people of Israel had been offering sacrifices to it. The bronze serpent was called Nehushtan.
> —2 Kings 18:4

Missing the essence

Essence is "the basic or most important idea or quality of something."[2] "The basic or most important idea" could be called the *core meaning*. When you're religious-minded, you get hung up on what God said and lose the core meaning—*why* He said it. When we as believers are copy-and-shadow-minded and lack revelation, we miss the essence of various scriptures and get stuck in ritualism.

Without discerning the core meaning, can you really obey God's intent? Perhaps, but you are much more likely to build a tradition around a misunderstanding or half-truth. Some of what happened to the children of Israel has spiritual meaning in the New Testament. However, some passages were fulfilled in Christ and not meant to be practiced in our churches, doctrines, and traditions, or incorporated into the believer's lifestyle. When the church structure is built around copies and shadows, the essence God is conveying is misunderstood.

Therefore, Jesus cut straight to the essence—the absolute basic, most important, and core meaning of His intent as expressed in Scripture: He said, "Do to others whatever you would like them to do to you. This is the essence of all that is taught in the law and the prophets" (Matt. 7:12).

Prayer shawls

The essence of Scripture is often missed where prayer is concerned. Among certain New Testament believers there has been a movement toward worship in a more Hebraic style. On the surface this approach seems harmless. However, I believe it indicates an internal struggle with orthodox Christianity and the embrace of a ritualistic, lifeless version of being saved. As if to compensate, some believers wear chains with the breastplate of the high priest, using it as an amulet to ward off demons or identify themselves as part of the Diaspora or lost tribes of Israel. Some read their Bibles by the light of a menorah, and some churches display large menorahs on the pulpit.

However, the Hebraic tradition that has gained the most traction with Christians is the wearing of prayer shawls. I am not anti-prayer shawl, but I will risk meddling with this "sacred cow." Use of the prayer shawl has become exaggerated and has moved beyond something God allows. Instead, it seems to identify Christian wearers as belonging to a particular class of believer. This is a distraction, a mild form of Israel's ungodly attachment to the bronze serpent Moses made. Can you wear a prayer shawl? Yes. But understand the connection between the shawl and the tendencies of deeply religious people.

Years ago in a season of deep consecration in prayer, I awakened at 5:00 a.m. each day to pray in my living room. Prostrate on the living room floor and wearing a huge prayer shawl, I would soak in God's presence for hours, often amid intense fasting for weeks at a time. This pattern continued for eighteen months, during which I had some of the most intense experiences with God and His Word.

During my prayer time one morning, I clearly sensed God asking me, "Do you think I listen to you more because you wear a shawl?"

I was about to say, "Yes, I do," but I wondered whether God's question was testing me. All I could say was, "You already know my heart. Wearing a prayer shawl doesn't make You listen more closely or draw me closer to You."

In that moment, I stood, folded my prayer shawl, and put it in a closet. I never used it again. And no—I'm not suggesting that you get rid of your prayer shawl. But if you believe you cannot connect to God without it, you will grieve the Holy Spirit, who guides you in prayer, with or without a shawl!

Missing the significance

When we miss the essence of Scripture, we fail to grasp the text's significance and deeper meaning, which are essential to the search for wisdom. Scripture tells us that wisdom must be sought; Proverbs 25:2 says, "It is the glory of God to conceal things, but the glory of kings is to search things out" (ESV). Elements within the Scripture text—characters, symbols, events, or themes—point to the deeper message and contribute to our accurate interpretation.

Are you struggling with legalism? If so, you are less likely to seek the deeper meaning of Scripture. Why? Because you've been taught deep meaning causes you to add to the text, something warned against in Deuteronomy 4:2 and Revelation 22:18-19. You might even fear that you'll end up in Gnosticism. (I not only feared that fate; I also warned other people about it!)

In reality, a child of God who is unencumbered by legalism can ask the Father questions. The religious mindset is a slave mindset, and slaves never ask questions. Therefore, spiritual slaves routinely miss significant truths God wants to reveal. When Jesus told His disciples He was going to die, "they didn't know what he meant. [His statement's] significance was hidden from them, so they couldn't understand it, and they were afraid to ask him about it" (Luke 9:45).

The disciples could not look deeper into Jesus' statement because their thinking restricted them from doing so. They simply could not process the idea of His death. However, they felt free to ask Him why He taught in parables. He answered,

> You are permitted to understand the secrets of the Kingdom of Heaven, but others are not. To those who listen to my teaching, more understanding will be given, and they will have an abundance of knowledge. But for those who are not listening, even what little understanding they have will be taken away from them.
> —Matthew 13:11–12

Don't miss the significance, if you can help it. Be willing to ask questions. The Lord answers!

Shofars

A timely example of missing the significance involves the Christian's use of the shofar, the ram's horn that the children of Israel sounded during various functions and battles. This Israelite custom is not a prescription for the church, however. I have nothing against shofars, but do we know why we are using them?

A famous Christian prophet was mocked on social media after trying to use the shofar in a prophetic act that went horribly wrong. (Blowing the shofar and producing its characteristic sound are not easy for the uninitiated.) Is it wrong to own a shofar? No. I own two of them. But I am wise enough not to blow them or interrupt a church service doing so.

This is not the place to explain the Old Testament uses of the shofar, but I suspect Christians use it because they want to copy what they see in the Old Testament. Instead of blessing the congregation, it causes disorder. Most often people use it without the pastor's blessing. They might mean well but are not considering the significance of what they are doing.

Before we move on, please pray this prayer:

> *Holy Spirit, I ask You to give me the essence and significance of the important points in this chapter of the book. Help me search them more deeply and see Your intent more clearly. In Jesus' name, amen.*

More Insight into Hebraic Customs

The rise in Hebraic forms of worship in Christian churches has been apparent for some time. Some people are acknowledging the Middle Eastern heritage of Jesus and the apostles. Others believe that simulating ancient or original forms of worship leads to more authentic worship. In reality, however, simulation is a copy.

Remember that legalism looks pious. But when legalism is added to any biblical truth, it stretches the original intent and forces extremism. This introduces conflict into the Christian life and makes our experience of freedom in Christ overly complicated. As we've mentioned, Galatians 3:21 says that there is no conflict between "God's law and God's promises." The verse adds that "if the law could give us new life, we could be made right with God by obeying it" (Gal. 3:21).

The desire to be more original and authentic has taken us to inauthentic places. Some churches believe we can't say the name *Jesus* because the Greek alphabet has no letter *J* (which is true but perhaps irrelevant). And because Jesus was Jewish, some have made a rule of calling Him *Yeshua* and avoiding the name *Jesus*.

These are examples of sincere believers being duped by copies. Once when my wife and I led a woman through a deliverance session, she took exception every time I said Jesus' name. That seemed odd enough, but as I continued, she started speaking in weird tongues and repeatedly screamed, "That's not His name. His name is Yahweh." Her seeming piety was actually a religious spirit that she "caught" on social media. So I rebuked it, and she got free.

There are other examples of Christians clinging to Hebraic ways. Some Christians are using Hebrew versions of their names. Others are greeting one another with shalom instead of hello. I even know a prophet who prophesies in sackcloth, like the two witnesses in Revelation 11. Some people believe that Elijah is one of these witnesses. And one day this individual told me, "I am Elijah."

I jokingly replied, "If you are Elijah, then I am Moses."

About a month later, videos appeared online, and guess what he was wearing? A potato sack and a belt made of rope. His seeming attraction to Jewish custom was a total veneration of Elijah. For the record, this prophet also comes from the extremely legalistic churches from which I came.

Please understand that these examples do not refer to true Messianic Jews who have come to the knowledge of Messiah and attend Messianic congregations. Even Messianic believers take issue with Gentiles trying to be Jewish. It's a matter of legalism leading to more and more copying of copies. Like a virus that keeps on spreading, there's never just one rule to obey. Always, the list of rules keeps growing.

Sectarianism as Consequence

Rigid rule keeping inevitably causes sectarianism, a divisive ideology that leads to intolerance, inspires violence based on religious or political differences, and causes people to dismiss other points of view. This divisive approach often results from not trusting the sufficiency of Christ Jesus or the reality of Him in every type and shadow.

This mindset blinds people to the essence of what God is saying and the reasons He used Moses to lead His people at a certain point in history. Because sectarianism is so virulent, it must be checked. Not surprisingly, Jesus rebuked His own disciples' sectarianism regarding an inhospitable Samaritan village:

> The people of the village did not welcome Jesus because he was on his way to Jerusalem. When James and John saw this, they said to Jesus, "Lord, should we call down fire from heaven to burn them up?" But Jesus turned and rebuked them.
> —LUKE 9:53–55

Intolerance can make loving believers (metaphorically) bloodthirsty. What made James and John think Jesus would appreciate their request? I believe it was connected to the Old Testament account of Elijah calling down fire in 2 Kings 1:10–12. The disciples misunderstood that event and imagined a connection to the situation they witnessed in Samaria.

We can easily become angry and venerate our viewpoints, which are often based on our speculation. Then we elevate these views to the level of doctrine. When we base our doctrines on types and shadows, sectarianism results. This is exactly what we saw with Westboro Baptist Church, whose aggressive demonstrations and harsh statements often made the news—in the name of evangelism, strangely enough.

When we as Christians call those with whom we disagree reprobates or children of Satan, we plainly declare that our brothers and sisters in Christ are unsaved or are false brethren. Many YouTubers spout these accusations, not out of holiness but out of sectarian anger.

Sectarianism has another nasty side effect: idolatry. Do you know anyone who started wearing a long beard after embracing the theology of John Calvin, or switched from contemporary worship to singing from a hymnal? There is nothing inherently wrong with adjusting your appearance to reflect those you honor as role models, but taken to the extreme, it might delve into idolatry.

The only person we are called to emulate is Jesus Christ. We are to "speak the truth in love, growing in every way more and more like Christ, who is the head of his body, the church" (Eph. 4:15).

Reverse Legalism

There is another kind of legalism we have not talked about: the reverse legalism that often plays out for those who have exited a religious environment. Once they break away, some people end up attacking anything that remotely reminds them of the churches in which they were raised. Suddenly, instead of mirroring the tabernacle of Moses or temple of Solomon, they try to make their churches look like modern theaters, stadiums, cafés, or studio lofts. Many antilegalistic churches don't even practice the Lord's Communion. They rarely preach repentance, and they carefully maintain seeker-sensitive environments with no mention of hell, the lake of fire, or condemnation. They focus on only the joyful aspects of the kingdom. They fail to snatch people from the fire, and some even swear that hell doesn't exist.

Breaking Free and Moving Forward

So how do we (1) break away from misunderstanding Scripture references that are types and shadows, and (2) recognize what they really represent, which is Jesus Christ? Here are some clues.

Reform without mercy for false doctrine

King Hezekiah handled the issue of the bronze serpent with the mindset of a reformer. He faced it head-on, regardless of the disruption it could cause. Reformers have no-nonsense goals and zero tolerance for playing politics. Hezekiah was bold, even destroying a relic that Moses had made. Some Jews saw the bronze serpent as a cherished reminder that Moses once lived. But for many, it became a stumbling block. Therefore, King Hezekiah intervened, ending the idolatry that had infected God's people.

For Hezekiah mercy was not involved. He was not concerned about those who were emotionally attached to the pole or dedicated their lives to honoring it. He simply cut out what he saw as a cancer.

To see reformation, we have to be equally bold. I've had some reservations in writing these chapters and have pondered whether I was going too hard on the subject. But no! Hezekiah's story encouraged me to keep writing. My purpose was not about having mercy for false doctrine; it was about calling out legalism and idolatry. Reformation demands choices that are clear and often difficult.

Rebuke with love

Reform also calls us to rebuke sectarianism, as Jesus did—with love. Rebuke the religious views that cause you to be divisive or antagonistic toward people whose views don't match your own. Rebuke this line of thinking, but don't condemn yourself or others in the process. The apostles whom Jesus selected sometimes displayed a sectarian streak, but Jesus didn't disqualify them. He corrected them.

Some churches try to slowly bring change but end up only rearranging the proverbial deck chairs. Why? Because they never issue rebukes. Jesus rebuked James and John swiftly. He made it clear He hated their way of thinking. We need to do the same.

Remember whose you are

Our part starts in recognizing who we are and whose we are. Consider the following passage of Scripture:

> You have not received a spirit that makes you fearful slaves. Instead, you received God's Spirit when he adopted you as his own children. Now we call him, "Abba, Father." For his Spirit joins with our spirit to affirm that we are God's children.
> —ROMANS 8:15–16

It took years for me to receive these words! I was servant minded instead of sonship minded. Because of the stifling legalism I experienced, I still struggle with this concept. I must constantly remind myself God loves me. If I don't, I will end up in the condemnation camp.

Let God break you away from being religious. Allow Him to

bathe you in the spirit of adoption that moves you from acknowledging God as your Creator (which is good) to receiving Him as your Father (which is even better). Your adoption came not by your righteousness but through Jesus' death on the cross. Take time to internalize the idea that while you were a sinner, Christ died for you! (See Romans 5:8.) And remember that God, your Father, loves you.

Someone who chooses to adopt you really loves you. You didn't choose God; by grace He chose you—when you had no good works to commend you. (See John 15:16.) And when you responded to His call, He gave you the spirit of adoption.

Be led by the Spirit

For too long too many of us have been led by rules and regulations. The rules give us boundaries and parameters, but they don't help us walk in the abundant life Jesus purchased. Being led by the Spirit is not ritualistic; it is a life of depending on and being intimate with the Holy Spirit. This is what pleases God. Even if the Lord has you following the rules, you will follow His leading. Forced behaviors and the fear of condemnation are not His way of leading you.

"All who are led by the Spirit of God are children of God" (Rom. 8:14). The spirit of adoption helps you live as a child of God, not just a servant. He gave you His Ten Commandments and other laws, but when you are led by His Spirit, you automatically do those things, through His power rather than your strength.

Intimacy with the Holy Spirit takes you from being driven to being led. Ask Him to help you fall in love with Him and follow His leading. Ask Him to reveal the deeper meaning of symbolism in the Scripture passages you read. He will show you! Look at what the author of Hebrews said about the duties of the Old Testament high priest and their deeper meaning: "By these regulations the Holy Spirit revealed that the entrance to the Most Holy Place was not freely open if the Tabernacle and the system it represented were still in use" (Heb. 9:8).

You are an heir of Christ

Finally, please know this: "Since we are his children, we are his heirs. In fact, together with Christ we are heirs of God's glory. But if we are to share his glory, we must also share his suffering" (Rom. 8:17).

When you truly realize you're a child of God, you quit striving to be or become, and you simply carry out who you are. You rest in Christ and enjoy the benefits of relationship with your heavenly Father. Any legalism is dissolved, and your inheritance is eternally secure. Rules and regulations cannot give you your inheritance or take it away.

> We have a priceless inheritance—an inheritance that is kept in heaven for you, pure and undefiled, beyond the reach of change and decay. And through your faith, God is protecting you by his power until you receive this salvation, which is ready to be revealed on the last day for all to see.
> —1 Peter 1:4–5

Chapter 11

THE PERFECT LAW OF LIBERTY

*Now the Lord is that Spirit: and where the
Spirit of the Lord is, there is liberty.*
—2 Corinthians 3:17, kjv

WE HAVE TRAVELED a long way together, and you may have already sensed that your freedom from legalism is not so much a supernatural encounter as a truth that needs to be believed. Immediately before Jesus said, "You will know the truth, and the truth will set you free" (John 8:32), He referred to what we might call heaven's constitution, meaning His teachings and our need to "remain faithful" to them (v. 31).

A Different Legal Mindset

Being free from legalism means learning and believing the truth from His Word. Paradoxically, the step toward your freedom is found in a kind of legislative mindset toward the Scriptures, which is oddly similar to how we embraced legalism. You can see the legislative mindset in the following statements from Jesus:

» "With what measure ye mete, it shall be measured to you again" (Matt. 7:2, kjv).

- » "Come to terms quickly with your accuser...lest your accuser hand you over to the judge" (Matt. 5:25, ESV).

- » "It is written" (Matt. 4:4, 7, 10, ESV). Jesus spoke these words as the devil tried to tempt Him in the wilderness. The devil also quoted Scripture; it was a courtroom deliberation, but Jesus won!

I believe the following words from the Book of James reveal the apostle's understanding of this legal mindset: He wrote, "The one who looks into the perfect law, the law of liberty, and perseveres... will be blessed in his doing" (1:25, ESV).When you understand the words *law* and *liberty*, they change your perspective. James is saying your freedom has been legislated by heaven's law.

This liberty is not an emotional, sensational experience that you must seek. But it involves a reformation of your theology—not a religious legalism but another legal system afforded to every believer by the efficacy of Christ's work on the cross. There is a massive clue in James's use of *liberty*. Notice that he didn't choose the word *freedom*. But why not? Aren't these words interchangeable? Well, no. Freedom refers to something more personal and relational; liberty is the legal word meaning freedom. This distinction places our freedom through Christ in a separate category where laws are guided not by feelings but by legislation. When Congress passes legislation, everyone is required to obey it, regardless of whether they feel like it.

Amazingly, legalistic Christians are ruled by a double-minded theology that mixes biblical truth with church bylaws. A legalistic person knows what the Bible says but generally prioritizes the bylaws that seem to blur theological lines. This happens because modern Christianity is very emotion- and experience-driven. Therefore, many are trapped in trying to feel truth rather than walk in it.

The apostle James moved the believer away from a promise-freedom mindset to a law-liberty framework. James is saying that we don't have to be enslaved to legalism. If we understand Christ's work on the cross, we are liberated from the rules and regulations, which we can never keep perfectly anyway. Redemption made it legally possible for us to stand fast. God's grace releases us from having to make ourselves holy and acceptable to God through legalistic addenda. We are already accepted in God through Christ. Therefore, our feelings shouldn't dictate us.

What I'm describing is a level of freedom that once seemed foreign to me. I thought I had to feel something, and if I didn't, I tried to force myself to feel it. But laws don't work according to feelings.

So how do we respond to the law of liberty? The following verses from James provide clues.

> The one who looks into the perfect law, the law of liberty, and perseveres, being no hearer who forgets but a doer who acts, he will be blessed in his doing.
> —JAMES 1:25, ESV

> So speak ye, and so do, as they that shall be judged by the law of liberty.
> —JAMES 2:12, KJV

We respond to the law of liberty by investigating it (looking into it), continuing in it (persevering), and speaking according to it. Let's see what all this says about how we are to live.

1. Look into the law of liberty.

James 1:25 tells us to look into the law of liberty. This requires some effort. While I served a nine-year prison term, many inmates used the facility's law library, a room filled with books describing cases that had been won or lost. Some inmates made it their business to look into the law. They searched volumes of case files, hoping to find one that resembled their own. Some inmates found information that helped them frame winning appeals that sent them home. But that would not have happened unless they looked into the law.

Those looking to break free from legalism have a similar task: They need to actively pursue the law—not of legalism but of liberty—wherever it can be found in Scripture. The Holy Spirit will highlight the information, but you must seek "first the kingdom of God, and his righteousness" (Matt. 6:33, KJV). There is a learning curve, but seekers learn how to navigate without the legalistic filter that once clouded their view. It's not easy. Fear often gripped me when I read verses about freedom in Christ. Why? Because I was trained to think freedom meant the license to sin, which it doesn't.

I'm going to give you one law of liberty that is foundational, but you will have to find others as the Holy Spirit guides.

Justification

The law I'll mention involves *justification*—a crucially important word that speaks to an essential element of what Jesus purchased for us through the cross.

> Therefore, since we have been justified through faith, we have peace with God through our Lord Jesus Christ, through whom we have gained access by faith into this grace in which we now stand. And we boast in the hope of the glory of God.
> —Romans 5:1–2, NIV

Through justification God moves you from a state of sin to a state of grace and righteousness. It's a judicial act that grants you complete absolution from guilt and releases you from the penalty of sin. When God imputes justification, it removes the burden of rules and regulations as standards for holiness. Justification by Christ *makes you holy*. You need only allow the Holy Spirit to empower you to walk out your justification, without worrying about measuring up to God's standard. Through Christ and His imputed righteousness, you measure up. This truth can free you, as it freed me!

2. Continue in the law of liberty.

Having learned about scriptural liberty, you continue by living it. Ask God to empower you to continue and not forget the truth, because if you forget, you will not continue. Remember that walking out what you are learning takes time. Like me, you will be tempted to slip back into old legalistic tendencies. And like me, you'll need to say, "Self, snap out of this legalism!"

Continuing is critical in moving from head knowledge to application and experiencing real results. If you catch yourself in a mistake, repent immediately and keep moving forward.

3. Speak the law of liberty.

Speaking the law of liberty reinforces your application of truth. I had to willfully allow these laws to permeate my speech, which had previously been filled with legalistic jargon. I was so judgmental and mean-spirited that I often offended believers who wondered how a pastor could be so brash. My wife often tried to fix the legalistic things I said from the pulpit or in conversations with members of the church. It took me many years to realize just how wrong my statements were. "Death and life [really] are in the power of the tongue, and those who love it will eat its fruits" (Prov. 18:21, ESV).

Your words can release God's power or violate the law of liberty, which is why James encouraged us to speak liberty. Once I challenged my legalistic language, the climate in our church services and culture shifted dramatically, and the Lord responded promptly.

Let the Holy Spirit guide your ways of speaking. The law of liberty actually mandates you to do so.

THE LAW OF WISDOM AND REVELATION

How do you grasp the law of liberty when your whole Christian theology is governed by legalism? The answer is *revelation*. Do you remember when Jesus asked His disciples, "Who do people say that the Son of Man is?" (Matt. 16:13). Peter responded, "You are the Messiah, the Son of the living God" (v. 16).

What an amazing moment that was! Jesus explained it by saying, "My Father in heaven has revealed this to you" (v. 17). Peter's response did not come from investigation but came from revelation. God revealed Jesus' identity because He wanted His people to receive grace and live under the law of liberty.

Remember that the Greek word *apokalupsis* is translated "revelation," which involves an unveiling or disclosure. There are hidden things God wants to unveil to you. He is not trying to withhold the revelation of grace or any other treasure of His Word. He is requiring you to seek Him with all your heart! This is essential because without revelation you can only regurgitate what you already know. This is why Sunday sermons in legalistic churches usually repeat and enforce the rules instead of emphasizing scriptural truths. Very little else is preached about Christ the person or Christ crucified, but what is said is labeled as holiness.

Can you see why having a revelation is essential to moving forward? Unless there is a revelation, what is said is nothing more than proselytizing. We can see this in the life of Saul of Tarsus. No one in the New Testament was more zealous for the Law of Moses and the tradition of the elders than Saul was. No wonder God had to personally knock him off his horse and give him a direct revelation! That revelation radically altered his perception of the Law of Moses and caused the early church to see that "the gospel of the uncircumcision was committed" to Paul even "as the gospel of the circumcision was unto Peter" (Gal. 2:7, KJV).

How did the Pharisee of Pharisees become the Apostle to the Gentiles? By revelation, as Paul himself explained:

> Dear brothers and sisters, I want you to understand that the gospel message I preach is not based on mere human reasoning. I received my message from no human source, and no one taught me. Instead, I received it by direct revelation from Jesus Christ. You know what I was like when I followed the

Jewish religion—how I violently persecuted God's church. I did my best to destroy it.

—GALATIANS 1:11–13

Paul was fanatical about his beliefs and, by his own admission, tried to destroy the church. To address the ignorance that once blinded Paul, God gave him direct revelation and called him to serve Jesus Christ and His church.

Although it is not coming directly from heaven like Paul's, my hope is that God is giving you revelation as you read this book. But you also need wisdom to know what to do with revelation. Wisdom enables you to apply knowledge, but with spiritual wisdom, you apply revelation. Revelation of the truth does not ensure God's intended outcomes, however. You can receive revelation from Scripture but mismanage it, which is why Paul prayed that God would give the church in Ephesus "the spirit of wisdom and revelation in the knowledge of [Christ]" (Eph. 1:17, KJV).

The revelations in this book will require you to pray for wisdom to live out what you are learning and then teach or preach to others. Wisdom will fill you with light, dispel any ignorance, and cause you to walk in the freedom Jesus purchased for you. So pray the following prayer to the Holy Spirit, asking Him to give you the spiritual wisdom and insight you need to understand and act on what you read about in this book.

> *Holy Spirit, I thank You for guiding me into all truth. I humbly ask You to give me spiritual insight, according to Ephesians 1:17. I ask You to _____. [Please complete the prayer in your own words.]*

WORSHIPPING IN THE DARK

The passage from Ephesians 1:16–18 shows that where there is no revelation of His Word, there is no light. But as the psalmist said,

"Your word is a lamp to guide my feet and a light for my path" (Ps. 119:105).

Without the light to guide you, you end up walking in the dark. Legalism produces believers who worship in the dark. That means everything is hidden and only discovered when you bump into it or listen very intently. Legalism emphasizes feeling because feeling and sound become your guides. Most legalistic churches and believers are loud and driven by experiences. They recognize rules but don't understand why God gave them. People worshipping in the dark have grown accustomed to it and even fight to protect it. That is why God wants to bring reformation.

Change in my life began with a revelation: God allowed me to see that He was trying to change my views. God's Word is powerful enough to shine in the dark places and lead you out, as He has led so many others. If you persist, you will move from the darkness of legalism into the marvelous light of revelation.

We can see the importance of revelation in two prime examples of how God upgraded the mindsets of His chosen vessels Abraham and Peter.

Abraham's second word

Abraham had the wonderful privilege of hearing God's voice so clearly he couldn't ignore it. When God asked Abraham to sacrifice his only son of promise, Abraham obeyed Him.

> Abraham picked up the knife to kill his son as a sacrifice. At that moment the angel of the LORD called to him from heaven, "Abraham! Abraham!"
>
> "Yes," Abraham replied. "Here I am!"
>
> "Don't lay a hand on the boy!" the angel said. "Do not hurt him in any way, for now I know that you truly fear God. You have not withheld from me even your son, your only son."
>
> —GENESIS 22:10–12

If Abraham had been legalistic about the first command God gave him, he would have dismissed God's voice the second time and would have killed Isaac. Many legalistic brothers and sisters who genuinely love the Lord will gladly lay down their lives in obedience to His commands. But often they miss the second command—the upgrade to their views or rules. The way God brought them to a certain point is not necessarily what He will use in the next phase of their journey. They need to hear what He says next and obey it, as Abraham did.

The apostle Peter's mindset upgrade

There is a dialogue between God and Peter that is probably my favorite because it is so clear. But God also spoke to a man named Cornelius, whose household would benefit from the revelation that Peter received from God three times. The vision concerned Peter's Mosaic mindset:

> The next day as Cornelius's messengers were nearing the town, Peter went up on the flat roof to pray. It was about noon, and he was hungry. But while a meal was being prepared, he fell into a trance. He saw the sky open, and something like a large sheet was let down by its four corners. In the sheet were all sorts of animals, reptiles, and birds. Then a voice said to him, "Get up, Peter; kill and eat them."
>
> "No, Lord," Peter declared. "I have never eaten anything that our Jewish laws have declared impure and unclean."
>
> But the voice spoke again: "Do not call something unclean if God has made it clean." The same vision was repeated three times. Then the sheet was suddenly pulled up to heaven.
>
> Peter was very perplexed. What could the vision mean? Just then the men sent by Cornelius found Simon's house. Standing outside the gate, they asked if a man named Simon Peter was staying there.

> Meanwhile, as Peter was puzzling over the vision, the Holy Spirit said to him, "Three men have come looking for you."
> —Acts 10:9–19

God communicated with Peter through the vision, but Peter couldn't understand what God or the vision meant. Why? Because Peter was still committed to the Law of Moses. Yet this passage shows that you can embrace a revelation even before you fully understand it! Just know that God's Spirit is guiding your steps away from legalism and toward the fullness of grace.

Peter was perplexed about the vision God gave him, but he obeyed and followed the men to Cornelius's house. I love that about Peter and am grateful he accepted the upgrade. This story was the most helpful one in teaching me to walk in God's grace even when I didn't quite understand what He was saying.

THE AMENDMENT AND SPIRIT OF GRACE

We talked about laws and commands, but let's talk about a required amendment for those who long to be freed from legalism: It's called the amendment of grace. Notice that "an amendment is a change or addition to the terms of a contract, law, government regulatory filing, or other documents."[1] Many legal systems allow for the changing of laws, as long as the changes are approved by whatever judicial agencies are appointed to oversee the process. But in certain kingdoms the king amends the laws to fulfill his sovereign purposes.

Similarly, God amended the law and chose grace through His Son, Jesus Christ. As a result, we now live in the dispensation of grace and truth. Grace is unmerited favor, the giving and receiving of what we don't deserve and cannot earn. In some sectors, the church has lost this great revelation. My prayer and hope are that the wonderful grace extended to us by Jesus Christ would be the dominant culture of our churches as the Holy Spirit, the Spirit of grace, continues to deposit grace in each believer's life at the point of conversion.

This empowerment is essential. You are not called to serve God out of fear; His grace covers you even when you fail. Breaking free from legalism doesn't mean you will be perfect. Legalism will creep in at times, but grace produces supplication to God, and He will empower you to repent and realign yourself with the Scriptures. Notice what Zechariah prophesied to God's people, who failed Him repeatedly:

> I will pour out a spirit of grace and prayer on the family of David and on the people of Jerusalem. They will look on me whom they have pierced and mourn for him as for an only son. They will grieve bitterly for him as for a firstborn son who has died.
> —Zechariah 12:10

God spoke these words long ago, but they also address a present reality for the church. Grace and supplication are dispersed to empower us to live free from the law while depending on the Holy Spirit, so we can cleave to the truth. The Spirit of grace is always present, and supplication is always available.

The Spirit of grace always fights the spirit of legalism and wins. Grace releases us from the prison of trying to please God by works. And it empowers our reliance on the sufficiency of Jesus Christ and His atoning sacrifice. Grace means receiving imputed righteousness in exchange for our sinful ways and attempts to appease God.

Salvation itself is a gift of grace and not works. The sooner you understand this, the sooner you will be released from the prison of besetting sin. Yes, you will sin, but you won't be overcome by it. Grace causes you to rise above sin and escape its mastery. "Sin will have no dominion over you, since you are not under law but under grace" (Rom. 6:14, ESV).

What to Do with Grace

The verse you just read makes me shout every time I read it. So let's take a closer look at the threefold way in which we respond to grace: First, we receive it. Next, we walk in it. And third, we depend on the Holy Spirit.

Receiving the grace of God

Second Corinthians 6:1 says, "We then, as workers together with him, beseech you also that ye receive not the grace of God in vain" (KJV). We receive grace the same way we receive salvation, yet many believers struggle to receive grace. And when we don't fully embrace it, grace is in vain.

I firmly believe our hesitancy is not a byproduct of conversion. New converts don't conclude that their faith must be upheld by legalism. They have no basis to believe such a thing. The idea is a programmed behavior passed on by well-meaning believers who learned legalism from other well-meaning believers!

Something that is vain is "marked by futility or ineffectualness."[2] A believer who hasn't received God's grace has difficulty producing results because empowerment comes with grace. Be sure not to mix the grace of God with legalism in your life. But first, lift your hands, and declare out loud that you are going to receive the grace of God and take it as your own. Please pray this prayer out loud:

> *Heavenly Father, I thank You for sending Your Son, Jesus Christ, to die on the cross and for exchanging my sin for Your grace. I receive the grace of God in my life right now. I repent for adding legalism to Your gift of grace. I renounce legalism in all forms. Holy Spirit, empower me to walk out this grace. Lord Jesus, _____. [Continue praying in your own words.] I ask You all these things in Jesus' name!*

Walking in the grace of God

After receiving the unmerited favor God grants through the death, burial, and resurrection of Christ, you are mandated to walk in it. You carry out God's grace in your daily living as unmerited favor empowers you to renounce "the desires of the flesh and the desires of the eyes and pride of life" (1 John 2:16, ESV).

The grace of God is not greasy or cheap. It's bloody: Jesus gave His life and blood for it. Grace gives us the desire to change so we renounce the unclean passions that once ruled us. "The grace of God that bringeth salvation hath appeared to all men, teaching us that, denying ungodliness and worldly lusts, we should live soberly, righteously, and godly, in this present world" (Titus 2:11–12, KJV).

The goal of the legalistic believer is to live a sanctified life. But it is God's grace that makes sanctified living possible. The Titus passage screams to every person who is trapped in legalism and says, "Grace is the key to holy living." By grace we no longer strive for holiness. We just walk in it, abiding in Christ through the power of the Holy Spirit.

Relying on the grace of God

Acts 13:43 says, "Many Jews and devout converts to Judaism followed Paul and Barnabas, and the two men urged them to continue to rely on the grace of God." Reliance on the grace of God is reliance on the person of the Holy Spirit. The apostle Paul admonished Jewish converts to lean on God's grace because he knew that as people trained in the Mosaic Law they would be tempted to trust in self-effort for their salvation.

If you are in this position, know this: Relying on the Holy Spirit means resting in and fully trusting Him. The righteousness of Christ is sufficient. Therefore, Jesus declared, "It is finished!" (John 19:30).

THE HOLY SPIRIT AND THE GRACE OF GOD

You and I are not left to fend off the cares of this life and the attacks of Satan in our own strength. The Holy Spirit is deposited into the believer's life so we can depend totally on Him. Jesus said, "The Helper, the Holy Spirit, whom the Father will send in my name, he will teach you all things and bring to your remembrance all that I have said to you" (John 14:26, ESV).

One of the ways the Spirit of God helps us is by enabling us to resist the spirit of religion. During moments of weakness, let the Holy Spirit remind you of Jesus' teachings regarding God's grace. You cannot walk in grace without the Holy Spirit coming alongside. When other legalistic brethren challenge your newfound freedom, you'll be sorely tempted to return to your old legalistic ways. But notice what Jesus promised:

> When the Spirit of truth comes, he will guide you into all the truth, for he will not speak on his own authority, but whatever he hears he will speak, and he will declare to you the things that are to come. He will glorify me, for he will take what is mine and declare it to you.
> —JOHN 16:13–14, ESV

The Spirit of God not only will transition your theology and point you back to Christ but will also glorify Him. Therefore, any tendency to deify or venerate legalism will lose its grip. Why? Because the Holy Spirit will glorify Christ, and "where the Spirit of the Lord is, there is liberty" (2 Cor. 3:17, KJV).

Breaking Free and Moving Forward

As this chapter nears its close, I offer you two powerful scriptures. May they encourage you to accept the grace God has freely given you!

> How much worse punishment, do you think, will be deserved by the one who has trampled underfoot the Son of God, and has profaned the blood of the covenant by which he was sanctified, and has outraged the Spirit of grace?
> —HEBREWS 10:29, ESV

May God give you more and more grace and peace as you grow in your knowledge of God and Jesus our Lord.

—2 Peter 1:2

Move forward, mistakes and all

Because I know how the insights I'm sharing have transformed my life, I trust the Holy Spirit to continue with you in this amazing journey. I'm cheering for you—and for myself because my journey is still underway. During this transition of grace, I have made many mistakes and foolish decisions. I have misunderstood many kingdom concepts and said some things I wish I hadn't.

And yet—the grace of God kept me, and He continues to lead me.

I said all that to say this: Do not let the habit of legalism demand perfection in your transition. You will have your moments. You will make your mistakes. Not all your decisions will be perfect. But you *are* advancing, and God will continue leading you. As long as you persist, you will break free from the grip of legalistic systems, and you will enter into the fullness of God's kingdom.

Stay open to revelation

As you move forward in your newfound revelation and understanding, the Holy Spirit will consistently increase your understanding in the grace of God. So stay open to what He says. Some of it will sound new or foreign to you because the ideas He presents will not be legalistic. The season of being manipulated is over!

Instead, His gospel of grace will heal and comfort you. It is the very thing you have unknowingly desired. And it is the aspect of His goodness that legalism tried to drum out of you. But the devil and his demons did not win. You are embarking on the journey of freedom in spite of them. Hallelujah!

Chapter 12

SAY GOODBYE TO BONDAGE

Stand fast therefore in the liberty wherewith Christ hath made us free and be not entangled again with the yoke of bondage.
—GALATIANS 5:1, KJV

LEAVING LEGALISM BEHIND is more than a change of mind. A level of spiritual warfare is involved. Not every difficulty is the work of demons, so I haven't yet talked much about the demonic. Yet demons are actively engaged in trapping believers in cycles of legalism. I have led people through deliverance when ugly demons of religion have surfaced. They are among the hardest, most stubborn demons to cast out.

Demons are bona fide legalists! Humans can violate heaven's spiritual principles, but demons do not. They cannot attack believers without either permission from God for some greater purpose (as in Job's case) or the opening of a door by the believer. Let's be clear, however: God isn't allowing demons of legalism—spirits specifically assigned to get believers to veer away from the grace of Christ toward a works-based gospel—to torment you. He will get the glory, and your testimony will help set other people free—potentially hundreds or even thousands of people throughout legalistic churches and denominations around the world.

So how do you discern when you're being oppressed by a demon of religion? What are the obvious and not-so-obvious signs? And how can you tell when the issue is a matter of bad theology, rules, or doctrines of demons?

Without being exhaustive, the answer is found in one word—*entanglement*. To entangle is to "weave" or braid.[1] You can't say goodbye to something with which you remain intertwined. It's like the old boyfriend or girlfriend who uses sweet talk to keep you from leaving the relationship: The attempt is both a sign of entanglement and a means of perpetuating it.

Seven Signs of Demons of Religion

In this final chapter I will describe seven entanglements that indicate the work of demons of religion—spirits assigned to keep Christians in false religions. My list is not exhaustive. However, based on my experience, this list covers the seven most prevalent experiences involving demons of religion.

1. Unregulated, counterproductive zeal

In chapter 5 we dug into the negative effects of unregulated zeal and how they relate to legalism. The person driven by unregulated zeal is not led by the Spirit of God. So this type of zeal is a sign, in my opinion, of demonic work.

When zeal is in the driver's seat, we forget to place our thoughts on the altar and check our alignment with Scripture before we open our mouths. Our desire should be to edify the church and bring glory to Christ. The Holy Spirit does not lead us merely to be heard or to gather attention. Paul was very plain about that, saying, "Forasmuch as ye are zealous of spiritual gifts, seek that ye may excel to the edifying of the church" (1 Cor. 14:12, KJV).

During Bible study in the prison chapel in 1995, I stood and started binding Satan out loud. I kid you not; I totally interrupted worship by walking up and down the aisles screaming at the devil to leave the service. You could say there was no clear sign of the devil operating in the service until I stood up in what I thought was an act of spiritual warfare.

I was nineteen and new to the faith. My heart was in the right place, but my actions were random and misguided. This was not a one-off situation. I had similar thoughts at other times, and they were overpowering. I fully believed they were coming from the Holy Spirit, but they weren't. Demons of religion were working my zeal and passion to produce unedifying and counterproductive actions.

Demons love drawing attention to themselves or tricking believers into following wrong voices. They know that your heart can be in the right place even when your methods are 100 percent wrong. That is what manipulation does, and demons know it.

2. Plaguing condemnation

Has condemnation overwhelmed you and caused you to believe terrible things about yourself? Condemnation can grip you during and after acts of service to God, and demons know just how to pull it off. If you're consistently plagued by condemnation, you are almost certainly being oppressed by demons.

Remember that Jesus Christ removed the guilt of condemnation by dying on the cross. Romans 8:1–2 assures us that "there is no condemnation for those who belong to Christ Jesus. And because you belong to Him, the power of the life-giving Spirit has freed you from the power of sin that leads to death." God dwells not in the realm of condemnation but in the realm of affirmation. He doesn't barrage you with thoughts of unworthiness or accuse you of not being "enough." Those thoughts are the specialty of Satan and his demons.

Are they saying your service to God is missing His standard of perfection? Are you self-condemning and self-critical? Well, that is *not* the Holy Spirit. Yes, He convicts us of sin, but He does not condemn us. (See John 16:8.) Demons, however, move in condemnation because they are condemned, and misery loves company.

3. Compulsive criticism

When you feel compelled to criticize yourself, other believers, or people outside the church, the devil is knocking on your door. Whether you get hung up on people's attire, spirituality, or opinions, you are being overly critical. This is a widespread issue in legalistic systems, and I have heard some of the nastiest criticisms being dished out there.

In chapter 3 I described how our church's Christian rap drew fierce criticism from other churches in our city. Some accused us of being a club and not a church, and they banned their members from attending any functions at our church. After that there was nothing I could do or say to change our critics' minds.

There should be space for people to disagree with us, but those who traffic in outright hostility are not Christlike. If you are harping on other believers because of differences in dogmas and bylaws, or if a woman in slacks makes your blood boil, God is not speaking through you. A demon is! Remember Jesus' own words and heed them:

> Judge not, that ye be not judged. For with what judgment ye judge, ye shall be judged: and with what measure ye mete, it shall be measured to you again. And why beholdest thou the mote that is in thy brother's eye, but considerest not the beam that is in thine own eye? Or how wilt thou say to thy brother, Let me pull out the mote out of thine eye; and, behold, a beam *is* in thine own eye? Thou hypocrite, first cast out the beam out of thine own eye; and then shalt thou see clearly to cast out the mote out of thy brother's eye.
> —MATTHEW 7:1–5, KJV, EMPHASIS ADDED

Years ago I needed deliverance from my judgmental thoughts against a particular denomination. I felt "called" to be the champion of Pentecostal theology, and I came down hard on my Calvinist brothers and sisters. I remember finally realizing I was compulsive in my interactions with them, so I embraced deliverance and got free from a division-loving demon of religion.

4. Hostility and contentiousness

Are you hostile toward those who view Scripture in ways that differ from what you believe? Are you willing to argue about it and eager to win them to your point of view? If so, consider this: Demons are often behind such quarrels and can cause a friendly disagreement to turn ugly fast. This dynamic is becoming prevalent among those with digital ministry platforms. They have been given ways to share the truths of God's Word via social media, but instead of propagating the gospel, they are picking fights. Some critics want to see other ministries exposed and shut down over these differences. Others declare that those who disagree with them aren't saved.

When such behavior erupts, a demon of religion is probably at work. James wrote, "If you have bitter jealousy and selfish ambition in your hearts, do not boast and be false to the truth. This is not the wisdom that comes down from above, but is earthly, unspiritual, demonic" (Jas. 3:14–15, ESV).

5. Attraction to legalism

This indicator of a religious demon never ceases to amaze me, particularly after seeing so many people who seemed to get free going back to legalism, even after many years. This reversal can happen for a variety of reasons. Sometimes life gets really tough, or a church or church leader stumbles. But sometimes the people who seemed to get free were not fully freed from demons of religion in the first place. Their seeming freedom may have been more behavior modification than heart transformation.

People return to all sorts of bondages for all kinds of reasons. One of the saddest situations is when a woman subjected to domestic violence leaves and later returns to a setting where violence is the norm. It's heartbreaking to watch, but it's not the Holy

Spirit's doing. Only the devil and his demons would cheer for that kind of misery.

If you previously fled from a harmful or debilitating situation but later subjected yourself to it again, I believe the devil is manipulating you. When I hear people say, "I miss that old-time religion" or "I need God to whip me into shape," I sense a demonic influence. When people shout amen after a very harsh sermon, I see the seed of legalism the devil placed there; it is alive and well and needs to be fully uprooted.

6. Extreme anger and rage

The source of extreme rage is easy to figure out: It is the work of demons! I'm about to confess something that I've never discussed with anyone but my wife, who witnessed my struggle and experienced its ripple effects. I knew how to polish myself for Sunday, preach the house down, win souls, and create an atmosphere in church. But at home I was filled with anger fueled by legalism. Yes, I was a Christian, and yes, I terrorized my family. On the outside I was calm, but when anyone broke the rules, all hell broke loose. One Sunday after church, I got so angry at my wife for breaking a church rule that I punched a hole in the bathroom wall. I am so fortunate my wife didn't pack up and leave me right then and there, because it was clear that demons had taken over my theology and ministry.

We were taught that legalism produces holiness, but it doesn't. It produces anger and rage. When I woke up the day after my outburst, I was very ashamed. I worked to fix the situation, but my dilemma was clear: I was extremely faithful to the rules and bylaws of the church but unfaithful to the law of love. I was under the impression—and was manipulated into believing—that the angrier I got about people not following the rules, the more I honored God and the vision of the house. I failed to understand the following scriptures:

> The wrath of man worketh not the righteousness of God.
> —James 1:20, kjv

> Be ye angry, and sin not: let not the sun go down upon your wrath: neither give place to the devil.
> —Ephesians 4:26–27, kjv

These verses remind me that issues with extreme anger involve demonic attacks in many (if not all) instances. We need to verbally renounce such demons and cast them out, praying along these lines:

> *Holy Spirit, I surrender and yield my emotions to You. Please close any doors opened in my life through anger that have given place to the devil. Satan and every demon of anger, rage, violence, extreme outbursts, and hostile temper, I command you in the name of Jesus to come out of my mind, come out of my emotions, come out of my body, and come out of my soul now. Go now, in Jesus' name!*

7. Distortion of Scripture

This final clue to the working of religious demons is tricky and often hard to detect. Demons are crafty. Some specialize in theology and know exactly how to hide behind it. First Timothy 4:1 says, "The Holy Spirit tells us clearly that in the last times some will turn away from the true faith; they will follow deceptive spirits and teachings that come from demons."

Demons that focus on theology trick believers into legalism by confusing or distorting their understanding of the Word. The primary assignment of these demons is to highlight the Scripture's stricter points. The goal is to cause believers to fixate on Old Covenant commands rather than on Christ. Biblical personalities such as Elijah, Moses, Daniel, and Noah become role models of Christian behavior instead of Jesus.

That statement might sound far-fetched, but our focus needs to be on Jesus, Jesus, Jesus. In legalistic circles sermons about God judging the children of Israel abound, however. I remember being taught about only Old Testament figures—*for years*. The devil capitalized on that arrangement, and I found myself emulating David instead of Jesus. I did not recognize my error until I left the legalistic system. And as I preached Christ-centered sermons, our church exploded.

If you are a pastor or leader whom God has called to preach, this seventh sign might be speaking loudly to you. Maybe you can't remember the last time you focused on Jesus instead of the patriarchs and prophets of old. But God wants to set you and your theology free from the demons that are pressing you and suppressing genuine kingdom revelation.

THE LAW OF FAITH

Saying goodbye to legalism requires something from you, and your freedom cannot move forward without it. The required element is faith! You have examined Scripture in these pages, and it has likely brought a measure of transformation. Why? Because "faith cometh by hearing, and hearing by the word of God" (Rom. 10:17, KJV). So let's explore faith's part in setting us free.

The Bible calls faith a law. Romans 3:27 says, "Where is boasting then? It is excluded. By what law? Of works? Nay: but by the law of faith" (KJV). Remember that laws are guided not by feelings but by legislation. If you enforce a law, it works. So the law of faith moves us away from feeling and presumption and toward freedom. And as Romans 3:27 shows, it is not a law of works.

Hebrews 11 defines faith as "the substance of things hoped for, the evidence of things not seen" (v. 1, KJV). Therefore, to appropriate your freedom from legalism, you must not rely on what your feelings say; you must instead apply the same measure of faith that first caused you to believe the gospel.

Why am I stressing the idea of not relying on feelings? It is because legalistic people live in the realm of zeal and emotionalism. The legalistic Christian experience is not confined to fixed rules and regulations. There must also be a heavy emphasis on emotionalism, which fluctuates. Emotionalism bypasses the ritualistic monotony of serving God, encourages a more vigorous system of man-made traditions, and diminishes or even cancels out true biblical faith.

Paul warned the Galatians that "the law is not of faith: but, the man that doeth them shall live in them" (Gal. 3:12, KJV). This verse is the silver bullet in destroying a works-based gospel. In His timing God allows us to not only read this verse but let it sink deep into our hearts where it brings transformation in the Spirit of our minds. (See Ephesians 4:23.)

Paul further helps us understand the connection between faith and grace in Romans 11:5–6 (KJV):

> Even so then at this present time also there is a remnant according to the election of grace. And if by grace, then is it no more of works: otherwise grace is no more grace. But if it be of works, then is it no more grace: otherwise work is no more work.

You are among those whom God has chosen to embrace the gospel of grace rather than a works-based gospel. The glorious freedom made possible by the death, burial, and resurrection of Christ is not about works but is accomplished through grace by faith. Even a slight addition of works dismisses or neutralizes grace.

ACCOUNTABILITY AND REGENERATION

Having read these pages, you are accountable to the truths they present. But I have great news: If you are coming out of legalism and saying, "I have no faith," don't worry! The Bible says that God has given each person who believes in Christ a "measure of faith"

(Rom. 12:3, KJV). God will use even a tiny mustard seed of faith that this book may have deposited so far.

The measure of faith within you equips you to understand what you are reading. A major truth that accompanies justification is the regeneration that occurs upon conversion to Christ. God regenerates your human spirit, which was "dead in trespasses and sins" (Eph. 2:1, KJV). You become one with Christ and are sealed until the day of redemption. (See 1 Corinthians 6:17 and Ephesians 4:30.)

Regeneration is "an act or the process of regenerating: the state of being regenerated."[2] One of the reasons regeneration is so important is that your regenerated spirit is essential to the process of becoming free.

As one of Christ's own you are no longer a servant trying to please a master who cannot be satisfied. No! As a child of God you are moved to obey Him through love rather than fear. Regeneration has changed your nature so that you are no longer among the "children of wrath" (Eph. 2:3, ESV). You are "a new creature" (2 Cor. 5:17, KJV). "Ye have not received the spirit of bondage again to fear; but ye have received the Spirit of adoption, whereby we cry, Abba, Father" (Rom. 8:15, KJV). Not only that, but "the Spirit itself beareth witness" with your spirit that you truly are a child of God (Rom. 8:16, KJV).

That is very good news!

Embrace Rest—as a Weapon

You have probably not heard of rest being a weapon, but it is. As a harsh, tiring taskmaster, legalism drains your rest. There is constant work to do, and there is always more work ahead. When I was in a legalist denomination, I spent many hours each day reading my Bible. Hours of Bible reading is not a negative, but doing it under compulsion is.

One day, I sensed the Holy Spirit prompting me to get out in the fresh air and rest. He seemed to be reassuring me that my Bible would be there when I got back.

I can guess what you're thinking: "Wait a minute! God told you to put down your Bible?"

Yes, He did. He knew I was so intent on reading His Word that I often skipped family functions, and I rarely enjoyed His beautiful creation. I stayed cooped up in my room day after day, reading and reading and reading. And sometimes I gave myself a headache! I had turned my Bible study into an arduous task I no longer enjoyed but felt compelled to do. I also spent long hours in prayer, and when I fasted, I pushed myself to the point of starvation.

Are you catching the pattern? Some of it came from a legalistic church I attended. Our worship celebrations and midweek Bible studies were in hyperdrive, with hours of extreme worship and emotionalism. Extreme worship was not the problem. But when the Holy Spirit wanted to move in a quiet or solemn way, our overzealous approach did not necessarily cooperate.

We were not satisfied to rest in God. Often, our church services were unnecessarily long. Many times we had what I called the after-party—a service after the service where we hoped to receive whatever we hadn't received during the "regular service." What we did was the opposite of rest: We tried to force everything. Legalism produced a lot of tired souls.

Jesus isn't interested in exhausting people. He's interested in loving and saving them.

> Jesus said, "Come to me, all of you who are weary and carry heavy burdens, and I will give you rest. Take my yoke upon you. Let me teach you, because I am humble and gentle at heart, and you will find rest for your souls."
> —Matthew 11:28–29

The enemy of your soul doesn't want you to rest from your works, your zeal, or your seeking of approval. Keeping you overly busy is a strategy of his because religion is a busy system. The passage we just read from Matthew 11 was Jesus' call to everyone exhausted by that system to come and rest in Jesus! He didn't say, "I will make you 'on fire' for God." He said that He would give you rest.

Rest is necessary. When you're rested, you are alert, sober, and vigilant. But if demons can keep you in ceaseless motion, Satan has a much better chance of tripping you up. I hate to say it, but some of the most legalistic believers who preach the hardest against sin are the first ones to fall into secret sins. No wonder God spoke about rest in Hebrews 4:

> So there is a special rest still waiting for the people of God. For all who have entered into God's rest have rested from their labors, just as God did after creating the world. So let us do our best to enter that rest. But if we disobey God, as the people of Israel did, we will fall.
> —Hebrews 4:9–11

The Lord also instructed the children of Israel to rest. As slaves all they knew was work. People locked in legalism are like overworked slaves. They need to know that God desires to give them rest.

The idea that Israel "rested from their labors" parallels God's rest on the seventh day. Resting from labor is not a sin. If God rested from His labor, we can rest from ours. In fact, God is requiring us to rest from legalism. If we don't, we are in disobedience. We need to do our best to enter this rest. In fact, we need a culture of rest in which legalism can't sneak up on us.

As you leave legalism, resting is your only defensive weapon. So ask the Holy Spirit to empower you to use it.

The Law of Confidence

One of the enemies that plagues people entangled in legalism is false guilt. I know firsthand how crippling it can be. False guilt tormented me nonstop and left me not a moment to rest. I wondered what would happen if I rested and missed the rapture or died and ended up in the lake of fire.

If I am honest, I spent the first fifteen years of being saved under a cloud of false guilt. It caused me to apologize to people "just in case" I did something that might have offended them. I also spent 90 percent of my prayer time asking God to forgive me of anything and everything I did that didn't please Him. I was afraid to have fun or go out and enjoy life. If I went out, I'd barely last a couple of hours before guilt made me run home to pray and read my Bible.

What I lacked as I tried breaking away from legalism was confidence in the biblical reality that I was saved by faith and not works. I also lacked confidence in the Holy Spirit's support in helping me serve God in a manner that pleased Him. Job 18:14 talks about a person's "confidence" being "rooted out" (KJV). The Hebrew word for *confidence* there is *mibtach*, and it means "trust, confidence, security, assurance."[3]

I was anything but what that definition describes. I came from the streets and a broken home. I lacked the ability to trust anything except rules and regulations. And I was riddled with false guilt. However, the tide began to turn when I read this passage:

> Jesus said to the disciples, "Have faith in God. I tell you the truth, you can say to this mountain, 'May you be lifted up and thrown into the sea,' and it will happen. But you must really believe it will happen and have no doubt in your heart. I tell you, you can pray for anything, and if you believe that you've received it, it will be yours."
> —MARK 11:22–24

The only way to move from unbelief to confidence is through the Word of God. The question, however, is whether we really believe what God has written. Personally, I struggled to trust His Word to free me from legalism. My spirit and mind were so contaminated with man-made rules, dogmas, traditions, and church superstitions that I had to remind myself that the source of Scripture was not men but God. Not only that, but to some degree I had lost even my faith in God. So I placed any faith I had left in my own strength. That is what legalism does!

GOD DOESN'T LIE OR CHANGE HIS MIND

Having faith in God is not the same as having faith in your faith or your strength. When I finally turned my faith back to my heavenly Father, the following revelation hit me: God doesn't lie or change His mind. In a world where the keeping of one's word has low priority, we have an unshakable truth on which we can rely: "It is impossible for God to lie" (Heb. 6:18). "Has he ever spoken and failed to act? Has he ever promised and not carried it through?" (Num. 23:19).

The idea of God's inability to lie gripped me! I dove back into the Scriptures with this revelation in mind, and my confidence in God grew. But God also wanted to show me something about Himself from a legal perspective. Before that I had only viewed Him relationally. Then I read the following passage and received a huge upgrade to my theology.

> God also bound himself with an oath, so that those who received the promise could be perfectly sure that he would never change his mind. So God has given both his promise and his oath. These two things are unchangeable because it is impossible for God to lie. Therefore, we who have fled to him for refuge can have great confidence as we hold to the hope that lies before us. This hope is a strong and trustworthy anchor for our souls. It leads us through the curtain into God's inner sanctuary.
> —HEBREWS 6:17–19

This passage thrust my confidence to another level. God knew that in a human sense I struggled with confidence for the same reason most people do: I'd grown up in an untrustworthy environment. In His infinite wisdom, He gave me an anchor of hope by saying He had bound Himself *with an oath* in the courtroom of heaven. Therefore, I could know and trust not only that He never breaks His relational promises but that He will never violate His legal oath.

The passage from Hebrews 6 still makes me want to shout! Because of all the revelation jam-packed into those verses, my lack of trust shriveled and my confidence soared. I realized the whole courtroom of heaven hinges on the fact that God cannot rescind His oath. He added an extra measure of trust by binding Himself in this way, and you and I need never lose our confidence again.

God bound Himself as our "eternal High Priest" (Heb. 6:20). He pledged Himself to those "who have fled to him for refuge" (Heb. 6:18). This same God will no longer count our sins against us but has placed them on His Son, Jesus Christ. And because of Christ's imputed righteousness to us, God will never count our sins against us. This nullifies the vexation of false guilt, long lists of external rules, and any form of works-based righteousness.

Our confidence booster is twofold: The Word of God is our legal constitution, and the New Covenant is the basis of our relationship with God. Look at what the apostle Peter wrote in regard to confidence after having seen Jesus' "majestic splendor with [his] own eyes" (2 Pet. 1:16).

> Because of that experience, we have *even greater confidence* in the message proclaimed by the prophets. You must pay close attention to what they wrote, for their words are like a lamp shining in a dark place—until the Day dawns, and Christ the Morning Star shines in your hearts.
> —2 PETER 1:19, EMPHASIS ADDED

When your mind is riddled with fear and anxiety as you pursue your grace-filled walk, remember what Peter and the writer of

Hebrews said. Peter's confidence soared because of what he witnessed, and the writer of Hebrews was anchored by God as the ultimate lawgiver. So whenever the devil and his cohorts try to tell you your walk of grace is really a license to sin, or being free in Christ couldn't possibly honor God, you can rest assured that your freedom doesn't rest on your work anyway. It rests on Christ's work and on the efficacy of God's Word!

Conclusion

My hope and prayer are that every trace of religiosity, formalism, and legalism will be eradicated from your life, and you will walk in the newness of life that Jesus purchased as your substitutionary sacrifice. Your new journey in grace is already underway, and the Holy Spirit has come alongside to help you stay grounded and focused on Scripture. Let Him motivate you to abide in Christ so you can bear much fruit. This freedom comes as you deny yourself, pick up your cross, and follow Him.

Your life from this point forward can be radically different, just as it was for Saul, who became the apostle Paul. After his conversion and by the power of the Holy Spirit, he broke away from the tradition of his forefathers, and he changed the known world. May you also play whatever part God has given you in changing the world as we know it.

And might Jesus' words—*It is finished!*—now be spoken as you turn away from the traditions of a legalistic system forever.

A PERSONAL NOTE FROM THE AUTHOR

God loves you deeply. His Word is filled with promises that reveal His desire to bring healing, hope, and abundant life to every area of your being—body, mind, and spirit. More than anything, He wants a personal relationship with you through His Son, Jesus Christ.

If you've never invited Jesus into your life, you can do so right now. It's not about religion—it's about a relationship with the One who knows you completely and loves you unconditionally. If you're ready to take that step, simply pray this prayer with a sincere heart:

> *Lord Jesus, I want to know You as my Savior and Lord. I confess and believe that You are the Son of God and that You died for my sins. I believe You rose from the dead and are alive today. Please forgive me for my sins. I invite You into my heart and my life. Make me new. Help me walk with You, grow in Your love, and live for You every day. In Jesus' name, amen.*

If you just prayed that prayer, you've made the most important decision of your life. All heaven rejoices with you, and so do I! You are now a child of God, and your journey with Him has just begun. Please contact my publisher at pray4me@charismamedia.com so that we can send you some materials that will help you become established in your relationship with the Lord. We look forward to hearing from you.

NOTES

Introduction
1. *Merriam-Webster*, "legalism," accessed June 3, 2025, https://www.merriam-webster.com/dictionary/legalism.
2. *Merriam-Webster*, "groupthink," accessed June 3, 2025, https://www.merriam-webster.com/dictionary/groupthink.
3. *Merriam-Webster*, "pietism," accessed June 4, 2025, https://www.merriam-webster.com/dictionary/pietism.

Chapter 1
1. *Merriam-Webster*, "strange," accessed June 4, 2025, https://www.merriam-webster.com/dictionary/strange.
2. WordReference.com, "concession," accessed June 4, 2025, https://www.wordreference.com/definition/concession.
3. Saul McLeod, "What Is Conformity? Definition, Types, Psychology Research," Simply Psychology, updated June 15, 2023, https://www.simplypsychology.org/conformity.html.
4. *Merriam-Webster*, "hermit," accessed June 4, 2025, https://www.merriam-webster.com/dictionary/hermit.

Chapter 2
1. *Merriam-Webster*, "veneration," accessed June 4, 2025, https://www.merriam-webster.com/dictionary/veneration.
2. *Merriam-Webster*, "veneration"; *Merriam-Webster*, "venerate," accessed June 4, 2025, https://www.merriam-webster.com/dictionary/venerate.
3. *Merriam-Webster*, "idolatry," accessed June 4, 2025, https://www.merriam-webster.com/dictionary/idolatry.
4. *Collins*, "brainwashing," accessed June 5, 2025, https://www.collinsdictionary.com/dictionary/english/brainwashing.
5. Encyclopedia.com, "Dogmatism," accessed June 5, 2025, https://www.encyclopedia.com/religion/legal-and-political-magazines/dogmatism.
6. "Westboro Baptist Church," SPLC, accessed June 5, 2025, https://www.splcenter.org/resources/extremist-files/westboro-baptist-church/; "Westboro Baptist Church Signs Stock Photos and Images," Alamy, accessed June 5, 2025, https://

www.alamy.com/stock-photo/westboro-baptist-church-signs.html?sortBy=relevant.

Chapter 3

1. *Collins*, "coercion," accessed June 6, 2025, https://www.collinsdictionary.com/dictionary/english/coercion.
2. *Merriam-Webster*, "opinion," accessed June 6, 2025, https://www.merriam-webster.com/dictionary/opinion.
3. *Merriam-Webster*, "groupthink."
4. Wikipedia, "groupthink," accessed June 25, 2025, https://en.wikipedia.org/wiki/Groupthink. Wikipedia cites multiple sources in presenting this definition.

Chapter 4

1. *Merriam-Webster*, "toxicity," accessed June 6, 2025, https://www.merriam-webster.com/dictionary/toxicity.
2. "Understanding Toxic Workplace Cultures," The Hive, accessed June 25, 2025, https://consultthehive.com/insights/articles/understanding-toxic-workplace-cultures/.
3. *Collins*, "literalism," accessed June 9, 2025, https://www.collinsdictionary.com/dictionary/english/literalism.
4. "What Is the Textus Receptus?," Textus Receptus Bibles, accessed June 9, 2025, https://textusreceptusbibles.com/What_is_the_Textus_Receptus.
5. Blue Letter Bible, "Strong's G4151—*pneuma*," accessed June 9, 2025, https://www.blueletterbible.org/lexicon/g4151/kjv/tr/0-1/.

Chapter 5

1. *Oxford Learner's Dictionaries*, "blasphemer," accessed June 20, 2025, https://www.oxfordlearnersdictionaries.com/us/definition/english/blasphemer.
2. *Oxford Learner's Dictionaries*, "persecutor," accessed June 20, 2025, https://www.oxfordlearnersdictionaries.com/us/definition/english/persecutor?q=PERSECUTOR.
3. *Oxford Learner's Dictionaries*, "insolent," accessed June 23, 2025, https://www.oxfordlearnersdictionaries.com/us/definition/english/insolent?q=INSOLENT.
4. *Oxford Learner's Dictionaries*, "insolent."

Chapter 6

1. Keith Miller, "12 Advantages and Disadvantages of Dictatorial Leadership Styles," Future of Working: The Leadership and Career Blog, accessed June 24, 2025, https://futureofworking.com/12-advantages-and-disadvantages-of-dictatorial-leadership-styles/.
2. Wikipedia, "Dictatorship," accessed June 24, 2025, https://en.wikipedia.org/wiki/Dictatorship#cite_note-FOOTNOTEGeddesWrightFrantz20183%E2%80%935-16.
3. Jack Kelley, "The Terumah Offering," Grace thru Faith, November 18, 2012, https://gracethrufaith.com/ask-a-bible-teacher/the-terumah-offering/; Wikipedia, "Tithes in Judaism," accessed June 24, 2025, https://en.wikipedia.org/wiki/Tithes_in_Judaism.

Chapter 7

1. *Merriam-Webster*, "distinction," accessed June 24, 2025, https://www.merriam-webster.com/dictionary/distinction.
2. *Merriam-Webster*, "adorn," accessed June 24, 2025, https://www.merriam-webster.com/dictionary/adorn.
3. *Merriam-Webster*, "respectable," accessed June 24, 2025, https://www.merriam-webster.com/dictionary/respectable.
4. *Merriam-Webster*, "modesty," accessed June 24, 2025, https://www.merriam-webster.com/dictionary/modesty.
5. *Merriam-Webster*, "propriety," accessed June 24, 2025, https://www.merriam-webster.com/dictionary/propriety.
6. *Cambridge Dictionary*, "preoccupation," accessed June 24, 2025, https://dictionary.cambridge.org/dictionary/english/preoccupation.

Chapter 8

1. Bible Hub, "602. Apokalupsis," accessed June 24, 2025, https://Biblehub.com/greek/602.htm.

Chapter 9

1. *Merriam-Webster*, "pietism."
2. *Britannica*, "Pietism," accessed June 25, 2025, https://www.britannica.com/topic/Pietism.
3. "What Is Pietism?," Modern Reformation, June 6, 2007, https://www.modernreformation.org/resources/articles/what-is-pietism.

4. *Britannica*, "Rumspringa," accessed June 25, 2025, https://www.britannica.com/topic/rumspringa.

Chapter 10

1. Wikipedia, "Shadow," accessed June 25, 2025, https://en.wikipedia.org/wiki/Shadow.
2. *Cambridge Dictionary*, "essence," accessed June 25, 2025, https://dictionary.cambridge.org/us/dictionary/english/essence.

Chapter 11

1. Will Kenton, "What Is an Amendment? Definition, How It Works, and Example," Investopedia, updated June 4, 2023, https://www.investopedia.com/terms/a/amendment.asp.
2. *Merriam-Webster*, "vain," accessed June 25, 2025, https://www.merriam-webster.com/dictionary/vain.

Chapter 12

1. Bible Hub, "1707. Emplekó," accessed June 25, 2025, https://biblehub.com/greek/1707.htm.
2. *Merriam-Webster*, "regeneration," accessed June 25, 2025, https://www.merriam-webster.com/dictionary/regeneration.
3. Bible Hub, "4009. Mibtach," accessed June 25, 2025, https://biblehub.com/hebrew/4009.htm.

SPECIAL THANKS

SPECIAL THANKS TO the following people God placed in the early days of my walk with the Lord and in ministry.

Thank you, Rev. Sergio and Elida Martinez, who were my first pastors when I came home from prison and allowed me to serve in ministry. I was rough around the edges, but your love for me helped me embrace the call of God on my life.

Thank you, Rev. Jean and Aleja DeLeon, who believed in God's call on my life and gave me the opportunity to preach my first sermon. Now I'm honored to preach to the world.

Thank you, Joseph and Guillet Pinero, my first copastors who served us faithfully when I first started in the pastorate. Twenty years later God has brought us back together. I am excited to see what the Lord has in store.

Thank you, Bishop Carlos Vega, for serving me in the early days of my pastorate and my work as an evangelist. We had many good times traveling from church to church, preaching and spreading revival.

Thank you, Evangelist Waldy Perez (United by the Fire Ministries). Together, we revolutionized New York City, and hundreds of young people's lives will never be the same. Your fire style of preaching always inspired me. Love you!

Thank you, Rev. Arline Vargas, for seeing the call of God on my life, ordaining me to the office of pastor, and appointing me to oversee my first church. You started me on a path that is expanding all these years later.

Thank you, Manny and Sylvia Maldonado. You have been with me from the early days of ministry and have seen every transition we've gone through. I wouldn't have gotten to where I am without your prophetic words. All of them have come to pass. Love you so much!

Thank you, Jonathan Escobar. We traveled together as evangelists and served as each other's best man. You were there when we started He Is Risen Tabernacle, and a lot of what we dreamed we would become has already happened. Neither of us would have started the process without the other. I miss you immensely!

Thank you, Pastors Luis and Yahaira Guzman. You both were there from the early days of my pastorate and served me faithfully with pure hearts. You both believed in me when I didn't believe in myself, and you covered for me when I was AWOL from the pulpit many times. Yet through all of it you remained patient and faithful as I matured. To see you both become pastors of your own church brings joy to my heart. You will always make me proud. Love you both!

Thank you, Nathalie Cabrera. Words cannot express how much I love you. You have always been the apple of my eye and my most faithful spiritual daughter! You have seen me trying to break free from legalism, and you walked with me every step of the way. No one was more faithful than you, which is why you will always hold a special place in my heart. You've had many spiritual leaders in your life, but you have only one spiritual mom and dad (and that's me and Ibelize)! To see you become a mighty woman of God and the wonderful mother of your own family brings us the greatest joy. We love you!

Thank you, Prophet Lourdes Lopez (Carlos Lopez). You came into our lives when I first started in the pastorate, and you entrusted your children to serve God in our church. Years later we're still together. It's safe to say that we will remain together until Jesus comes. I love you.

Thank you, Gabriel Martinez. You were there when I was ordained an evangelist. You were there when I became a pastor. And you were there when God called me to be an apostle. You are the embodiment of what it means to be loyal, and though the enemy tested it for a couple of years, you came back home. Love you and the kids. Erica is amazing!

ABOUT THE AUTHOR

ALEXANDER PAGANI IS the founder of Amazing Church in the Bronx, New York. He is an apostolic Bible teacher with keen insight into the realm of the demonic, generational curses, and deliverance. An internationally sought-after conference speaker, he takes an uncompromising approach to the Scriptures and has been involved in more than four hundred deliverance sessions. He has appeared on various television networks, including TBN and The Word Network. An honorary graduate of Central Pentecostal Bible Institute, he carries a spirit of wisdom and discernment to unlock secrets of the kingdom, with signs and wonders following his ministry. Pagani is the best-selling author of *The Secrets to Deliverance* and was featured in the 2023 film *Come Out in Jesus Name*. He and his wife, Ibelize, have two sons, Apollos and Xavier, and live in the Atlanta area.